Copyright © 2024 by author Russell James Verhey
All rights reserved.

All rights reserved, including the right of reproduction in whole or in part in any form without prior permission of the publisher, except as provided by USA copyright law. To contact the publisher, please visit www.spiralingupleader.com.

Published by
Wisdom Way
Colorado Springs, Colorado

Cover design: Double Studios #optimalgraphics
Interior layout: Marcus Costantino, LLC
Cover photo: Ashlee Kay Photography, www.ashleekay.com

ISBN-13 (hardcover): 979-8-9916474-0-3
ISBN-13 (softcover): 979-8-9916474-1-0

First Printing, 2024
Printed in the United States of America

Spiraling Up is a must-read for leaders seeking a well-structured blueprint for building a positive and thriving company culture. This book provides well-researched theories combined with practical strategies and actionable team-building activities that will resonate with leaders across all industries. With a unique blend of empathy, authenticity, and strategic know-how, Dr. Verhey offers a comprehensive framework to combat negativity, boost morale, and foster a positive, productive environment. If you're ready to take your leadership and organization to the next level, *Spiraling Up* is the guide for which you've been waiting.

Mike Cleveland, President and COO, phData Inc.

Russell's book is a game-changer for those struggling with negativity within their workplace. It is a practical guide that can help you navigate and overcome the challenges of negativity. Negativity can damage so many areas of life if not handled correctly. That is why this book is such a blessing. It is well-written and thought-provoking. Russell does a great job balancing practical application with theory. It is a must-read.

Aaron Ramsay, CEO, Envision Radiology

The antidote for the rampant contagion of negativity plaguing our workplaces may just be found in this smart, practical read.

Bruce Williamson, VP of Marketing, Compassion International

Russell Verhey's insightful approach to defining and building positivity in the workplace is unique and timely – and a must-read for any leader who desires to create meaningful impact. Every leader in every organization must navigate their emotions, and those of their team members, while achieving results. By combining the science of how we humans think, feel and operate with memorable storytelling, Russell has delivered to us a playbook for rethinking leadership, organizational culture, and driving change.

Mollie Bell, Chief Development Officer, Ent Bank

Harnessing both scientific research and practical experience, Russell Verhey shows us how to break the trance of the negativity bias to unleash positive potential within organizations. In *Spiraling Up* we learn how culture practices like appreciation, playfulness, and authentic human connection are not just 'feel-good'; rather, they are integral to the organization's capacity to sustain success and do big things.

Christina Congleton, Ed.M., PCC, Author of Getting Over Ourselves

Spiraling Up will help to unlock the full potential of your team and create a thriving, positive workplace. Dr. Russell Verhey provides powerful and practical insights, guiding readers through understanding negativity, addressing it with effective strategies, and implementing practical steps for lasting change. With dedication, compassion, and a steadfast commitment to positive change, leaders can transform even the most challenging workplace dynamics to create organizations that thrive in adversity.

Heather Zweifel, Chief People Officer, Journey Construction

CEOs and leaders struggle with personal and business negativity every day. It's grind to lead through, especially if you don't know how to attack it at the core. *Spiraling Up* provides all business leaders practical and approachable techniques to identify and combat negativity in all its forms to build a better culture, improve outcomes, and impact the lives of those we serve.

Dan Cooper, CEO, Acumen

When negativity becomes a cycle in our organizations, leaders have a choice to make. Dr. Verhey presents authentic leadership as a strategy by compiling examples of leadership lessons from his own research and others. The result is a framework to inspire leaders to ask meaningful questions to reshape a positive culture and "Spiral Up." Complete with powerful narratives and practical exercises, leaders who feel the sense of urgency to combat toxicity will have a roadmap with this book.

Brigit Olsen, PhD, Industrial-Organizational Psychologist and Consultant

"A LEADER'S RESPONSE TO
NEGATIVITY IN THE WORKPLACE"

SPIRALING
UP

DR. RUSSELL VERHEY

Contents

Foreword	IX
Spiraling Up: Author's Journey	XI
Introduction	XIV
PART 1: Understanding Negativity in the Workplace	1
1. The Nature and Impact of Negativity Bias	3
2. The Role of Leadership in Shaping Workplace Culture	21
PART 2: The SPIRAL 6-Step Framework for Transforming Negativity	37
3. Step 1 - Strengthen Authentic Leadership	39
4. Step 2 - Pinpoint Negativity's Impact	55
5. Step 3 - Influence Positive Mindsets	69
6. Step 4 - Rebuild Psychological Capital	85
7. Step 5 - Address Negativity Constructively	99
8. Step 6 - Leverage Positivity and Celebrate Success	113
PART 3: Putting It All Together	133
9. Leading the Transformation - A Holistic Approach	135
10. Spiraling Up - Sustaining a Positive Workplace Culture	155
11. Final Thought - Be the Catalyst for Change You Hope to See	169
12. Bonus Chapter - The Positivity Flywheel	173

Appendix I: Definition of Terms	187
Appendix II: Executive Interview Profile Chart	193
Appendix III: Pre-work Questions for Consulting Engagement	195
References	197
Acknowledgements	207
About the Author	209
Leaders Advance	211

Foreword

It can be hard enough for an organization to deliver results, much less adapt to survive and thrive in today's fast-paced, ever-changing world. But, as leaders, often we must both perform and transform simultaneously. We must execute with excellence today and be relevant to exist tomorrow. To do so takes insights, strategy, courage, resilience as an organization, as individuals, and as a team.

As a strategist, it's no surprise that I love a good insights-based strategy that leverages an organization's unique assets to create value that stands out vs the landscape of alternatives. But strategy isn't enough; it is just the beginning. Peter Drucker had it right when he famously said, "Culture eats strategy for breakfast." Getting the culture right is a critical enabler to breathe life into your strategy to create value and unlock your organization's potential.

The good news is that in work organizations, you are not stuck with the culture that you have. Culture can be transformed, and indeed needs to be transformed to maximize impact of the important work that your organization does. The work of culture change is hard but worth it, as the dividends are huge. Not only will a better culture deliver better results, but it is a lot more fun and rewarding to work there and can improve the lives of the many people whom your organization touches.

But how do I get started with culture change? If you are in trouble and your organizational culture is spiraling down in a crisis requiring immediate intervention, Spiraling-Up is like a "break glass in case of emergency" kit. It is packed with thoughts, ideas, and exercises that you can apply to an organization today, too. Or maybe you realize the importance of people and culture, have the motivation, but are just not sure where to start. Some of us don't have a PhD in neuroscience or organizational psychology to figure out what is going on with our people and organization. Spiraling Up can walk you through the step-wise framework to begin the culture change journey. Others don't have the budget and resources to hire and engage with consultants to figure it out, much less implement a plan. Spiraling Up can help you understand the levers of culture change you can start to engage in today.

Sometimes, the challenge is that you don't understand how important you are as a leader. You matter. People are watching you more than you think. Every decision, what you value, how you treat people, and every action that you take is a thread that becomes part of the tapestry of your organization's culture. You can make a difference. As a leader, you set the tone for the culture in your work group, your division, or your organization. It is your privilege, honor, and responsibility to lean in and actively shape the culture or organization. Culture transformation is hard work, but it is worth it.

Michael Brunner
Senior Director R&D Strategy at Kimberly-Clark

Spiraling Up: Author's Journey

IMAGINE WALKING INTO A room where everyone knows you have been hired help a team of leaders improve their organization. There is tension in the air. Skepticism. Maybe even cynicism. And it is your job to not only guide the organizational transformation, but also the individuals who will be responsible for implementing it, those staring you down.

As an organizational development consultant, I partner with leaders to resolve conflicts and improve teamwork. Being the outsider is common for me. On this day, as I embraced my first interaction with a group of doctors and nurses, I was not surprised by the lack of hospitality. I had barely begun when one physician's voice cut through the air as he physically slapped his hand on the table, "What are you saying, Russell, that we are supposed to be a team?"

After his outburst, the room went quiet. I could sense the frustration and disillusionment in the room. At that moment, I realized the enormity of the challenge before me. These highly educated, ostensibly professional individuals were acting like squabbling children. It struck me that this scenario was all too familiar. From grade school to corporate boardrooms, we're often thrust into groups we don't choose, filled with people we may not particularly like.

As I scanned the faces of the group, their hostility was evident. I soon learned each had retreated into their silo, refusing to engage with their colleagues on even the most essential issues. As I worked with them collectively and individually, most attempts at soliciting feedback or new ideas was met with fierce resistance.

The toxicity had seeped through every level of the organization. The results were measurable. Experienced nurses were on the brink of quitting. Patient satisfaction scores were plummeting due to scheduling chaos and long wait times. The effects of burnout permeated the entire staff. At the top, executives were sounding the alarm, but instead of solutions, they found only a vicious cycle of blame. The physicians pointed fingers at the administration's demands, while no one dared to take responsibility for the mess they'd created.

What would you do in this situation? What would go through your mind?

Where to begin? To be able to reverse the negativity into a positive workplace culture.

As a veteran business owner and leadership consultant, I've witnessed firsthand the insidious effects of workplace negativity—a silent killer of productivity, creativity, and morale. This negativity can manifest in various ways, from toxic gossip and backstabbing to a lack of trust and respect among team members. I've seen vibrant workplaces transform into soulless environments where employees merely clock in and out, devoid of joy or fulfillment. The impact ripples far beyond individual well-being, creating a revolving door of turnover that threatens organizational stability and success. As someone deeply passionate about seeing people thrive in work and life, I found this situation unacceptable and deeply personal. This is not just a professional concern but a personal one.

But here's the silver lining: just as we choose negativity, we can also willingly take its antidote. I have researched, witnessed, and implemented the transformative power of positive change. I've partnered with courageous leaders to reshape toxic cultures into thriving environments where employees feel valued, engaged, and empowered. These experiences have shown me that a positive workplace isn't just a nice-to-have perk—it's a crucial driver of organizational success and individual fulfillment.

"Spiraling Up" is not just a book; it's a leadership guidebook that I've authored based on years of hands-on experience, rigorous academic research, and deep conversations with leaders on the front lines. It provides practical strategies and tools to combat workplace negativity, blending leadership and psychological theory with insights from over 100 social and psychological workplace studies, validated by the firsthand experiences of a dozen CEOs and executives grappling with negativity in their organizations.

Join me as we explore how to turn the tide, transforming your workplace from a breeding ground of pessimism into a beacon of positivity and productivity. Your active participation and commitment are not just crucial, they are integral in this journey. Your journey towards a more positive workplace starts here.

Let's spiral up together.

Russell Verhey

Introduction

A Leader's Journey to Transforming Workplace Negativity

I HAVE LEARNED IN fifty-plus years of life that you are one click, one call, or one conversation away from negativity pulling you down into a miry pit. How do you respond when negativity comes knocking at your door? Hopefully, your home is a haven from some of the tyranny of the day. Life holds many challenges without having to look for them. Ideally, going to your place of work should be a positive, productive environment where some levels of professionalism shield people from a toxic culture. However, as a business owner for fifteen years and a consultant for the past decade, coaching nearly 500 leaders, I have had a front row seat to the debilitating effects of workplace negativity. This personal experience has not only given me a deep understanding of these challenges but also a profound empathy for those who bear the brunt. From my early days as an entrepreneur, I grappled with managing difficult personalities, resolving conflicts, and fostering a positive team dynamic in the face of adversity. These experiences ignited a passion in me to understand the root causes of workplace negativity and develop effective strategies for leaders to combat it.

Throughout my years of coaching and consulting, I have seen negativity manifest in countless ways across organizations of all sizes and industries. Whether it takes the form of toxic gossip that poisons team relationships, cynicism that stifles innovation, resistance to change that hampers progress, or outright hostility that creates a volatile work environment, negativity can quickly spread like a virus, infiltrating teams, and eroding the very foundation of a healthy, productive workplace. I have witnessed the toll that unchecked negativity can take on employee morale, engagement, and mental health, as well as its devastating impact on organizational performance and bottom-line results.

Yet, amidst these challenges, I have also had the privilege of working with remarkable leaders who have survived and thrived in the face of workplace negativity. These leaders, with their unique combination of authenticity, emotional intelligence, and strategic savvy, have shown that it's possible to confront negativity with compassion, clarity, and unwavering resolve. Their stories and insights have inspired me and ignited a fire to decode the secrets of transforming negative workplace dynamics.

The Need for Immediate Action: Addressing Negativity and Creating Positive Work Environments

My passion for empowering leaders to create positive, thriving organizations has led me to pursue a doctoral dissertation on executive leaders' responses to negativity in the workplace. My research involved in-depth interviews with seasoned executives across various industries, including banking, education, healthcare, manufacturing, construction, and non-profit, where I sought to uncover the key strategies, mindsets, and practices that distinguished those leaders who could effectively combat negativity and cultivate a culture of positivity, trust, and collaboration. The insights from this research and my extensive experience coaching leaders on the front lines of organizational change form the foundation of *Spiraling Up*.

This book is the culmination of my research findings and extensive coaching experience; it is a distillation of the most powerful, practical insights and techniques for understanding, addressing, and transforming workplace negativity. *Spiraling Up* is a comprehensive roadmap for leaders at all levels committed to driving positive change in their organizations, promising to revolutionize their approach to leadership and organizational culture; this path toward well-being is encapsulated withing an acronym, SPIRAL, a 6-Step Theoretical Framework designed to empower leaders with a simple, memorable, and clear approach to foster positive organizational change. Each letter represents a crucial step:

1. Strengthen Authentic Leadership
2. Pinpoint Negativity's Impact
3. Inspire Positive Mindsets
4. Rebuild Psychological Capital
5. Address Negativity Constructively
6. Leverage Positivity and Celebrate Success

This carefully crafted sequence guides leaders through a transformative process, encouraging them to cultivate authentic leadership, recognize and mitigate negative influences, promote positivity, build resilience, constructively manage challenges, and reinforce positive outcomes. By following the SPIRAL framework, leaders can effectively communicate and implement a strategy for "Spiraling Up," creating a more positive, productive, and resilient organizational culture.

As someone who has been in the trenches of organizational leadership and witnessed both the devastating impact of unchecked negativity and the transformative power of positive, proactive leadership, I am deeply committed to sharing these insights with leaders ready to take their organizations to the next level. By embracing the principles and strategies outlined in this book, leaders can combat workplace negativity and improve employee morale, increase engagement, enhance mental health, and boost organizational performance. Leaders can become catalysts for positive change, creating ripple effects extending far beyond their immediate teams and organizations.

Making the Most of Spiraling Up: Begin Where Your Organization Needs Your Leadership

While traveling with Mike, president of a software engineering organization, to his executive team building offsite in Minneapolis, he asked an insightful question: "How do I proactively prevent negativity and identify blind spots? We have a positive culture today, but I want to uncover and address any issues as early as possible." This proactive approach exemplifies the mindset needed to maintain and enhance a positive organizational culture. The SPIRAL 6-step framework provides a roadmap for culture change. However, it's essential to recognize that organizations are at various stages in their cultural journey. You may have already made significant strides towards fostering a positive culture. The key is identifying gaps in your leaders, teams, departments, and the organization.

Scan to Take the PLX

When implementing the "Spiraling Up" approach, assess your leadership and organization's positivity score. Based on your Positivity Leadership Index (PLX), this baseline assessment will guide you through the Spiraling Up outline, indicating where you can lean into each chapter for insights and action steps. The PLX provides a brief analysis to pinpoint areas of strength and potential vulnerabilities. Further data research may involve employee surveys, focus groups, or external audits. Once you've identified these areas, you can tailor the implementation of the framework to address your specific needs. This flexible approach allows for a customized strategy that addresses your unique challenges and builds on your strengths. A positive culture change initiative's main goal is to bolster alignment, productivity, engagement, morale, retention, and customer satisfaction, ultimately influencing the bottom line. By focusing on the areas where your organization needs leadership most, you can maximize the impact of the "Spiraling Up" framework and create lasting positive change.

As you embark on this journey, remember that cultural change is not a one-time event but an ongoing process. Regularly reassess your progress, retake the PLX, celebrate your successes, and be prepared to adjust your approach as needed. By staying vigilant and proactive, you can prevent negativity from taking a toll and create a thriving, resilient organizational culture that propels your business forward.

Overview of the book's purpose and structure

Whether you are a seasoned executive looking to reinvigorate a stagnant culture or a new manager seeking to build a foundation of positivity from the ground up, 'Spiraling Up' is designed to be your guide, your toolkit, and your inspiration on this transformative journey. The book is divided into three parts: Part 1 focuses on understanding workplace negativity, Part 2 delves into the SPIRAL strategies for addressing it, and Part 3 provides practical steps for transforming it. Each chapter will be concluded with a summary of insights, reflection questions, and a team exercise, creating a real-time response for leaders with their teams. Together, we will explore the art and science of authentic leadership, the power of reframing negative mindsets, and the practical steps you can take to cultivate a workplace culture that brings out the best in everyone.

So, let us embark on this journey together as we uncover the secrets of "spiraling up" and unlock the full potential of our teams, our organizations, and ourselves as leaders in an ever-changing world. With your dedication, compassion, and steadfast commitment to positive change, we can transform even the most challenging workplace dynamics and create organizations that thrive in adversity.

PART 1:
Understanding Negativity in the Workplace

Chapter 1
The Nature and Impact of Negativity Bias

A S I WRITE THIS chapter, my mind is flooded with countless stories of the pervasive challenges of toxic workplace cultures, demoralized employees, and leaders struggling to combat negativity. Your challenges may feel unique and isolated, but as a front-line organizational consultant, I can attest that these issues span industries and all levels of organizations:

1. Perioperative nurses battling with complex physician relationships
2. Construction field superintendents maintaining composure while facing demanding office expectations
3. Product managers pushing back against unrealistic delivery goals from their executives
4. A plant manager nearing burnout while running three shifts, battling high turnover, and facing pressure from new ownership to increase output
5. A discouraged executive team reeling after a heated board meeting due to missed fourth-quarter numbers

There are countless of these wide-ranging symptoms influencing overwhelming waves of negativity felt across organizational levels and sectors. My decades of experience and research have crystallized the urgent need to confront one of the most insidious threats facing organizations today: negativity bias. And I believe the effects after the pandemic have only magnified and exacerbated this plunge into negativity.

At its core, negativity bias refers to our human tendency to give greater psychological weight to negative experiences, emotions, and interactions than to positive ones. It's a survival mechanism that once served us well. Still, it can become a destructive force in the modern workplace, eroding trust, stifling innovation, and undermining even the most well-intentioned leadership efforts.

In this chapter, we'll explore the pernicious nature of negativity bias and its genuine impacts on individuals, teams, and entire organizations. Drawing from research in psychology and organizational behavior and real-world case studies shared by the executives I interviewed, we'll paint a vivid picture of how unchecked negativity can sabotage employee well-being, productivity, and retention. Most importantly, we'll make the case for why addressing negativity bias must be a top priority for any leader committed to building a thriving, resilient organization. As one executive said, "If you don't address negativity, it builds and feeds until it starts to become the expected norm." This chapter is a wake-up call and a rallying cry - a challenge to confront negativity head-on and cultivate a more positive, productive workplace culture.

Spiraling Effect

The spiraling effect within organizational contexts, whether positive or negative, is a priority focus. Scaling downward requires urgency, as it requires immediate attention to mitigate risks, whereas spiraling up is aspirational, guiding the organization toward the desired cultural state. The profound and far-reaching consequences of negative spirals for individuals, teams, and entire organizations cannot be overstated. Fredrickson's (2001) broaden-and-build theory of positive emotions provides a framework for understanding these spirals, suggesting that positive emotions broaden one's thought-action repertoire while negative emotions narrow it. When spiraling down, negative experiences and feelings can create a self-perpetuating cycle of further negativity, leading to decreased motivation, reduced productivity, and deteriorating relationships.

At the individual level, negativity bias can amplify the impact of negative experiences, making them more salient and memorable than positive ones (Rozin & Royzman, 2001). This can trigger a cascade of negative thoughts and emotions, potentially leading to increased stress, anxiety, and even depression. Nolen-Hoeksema's (1991) response styles theory suggests that rumination on adverse events can prolong and intensify depressive episodes, creating a self-reinforcing cycle of negativity. In the workplace, this might manifest as an employee becoming increasingly disengaged, pessimistic, cynical, and resistant to change.

The spiraling-down effect can be equally detrimental at the team and organizational levels. Felps et al. (2006) examined the impact of negative team member behaviors such as constant criticism, lack of cooperation, or disruptive behavior on group processes and performance, finding that a single 'bad apple' can significantly decrease overall team functioning. This negative influence can spread through emotional contagion (Barsade, 2002), where negative moods and behaviors are unconsciously mimicked and internalized by others. Over time, this can lead to a toxic organizational culture characterized by low morale, high turnover, and decreased innovation. Sutton's (2007) work on the 'no asshole rule' highlights how unchecked negative behaviors can poison entire work environments, creating a self-reinforcing cycle of negativity that becomes increasingly difficult to break.

Given the potent and pervasive nature of negative spirals, there is a critical need to develop strategies for reversing this trend and fostering upward spirals of positivity. Fredrickson and Joiner's (2002) research suggest that positive emotions can trigger upward spirals of emotional well-being, broadening cognitive perspectives and building personal resources. This underscores the potential for positive change in organizational contexts. Leaders play a crucial role in this process, as their behaviors and attitudes can significantly influence the emotional climate of the workplace (Avo-

> Negativity is not just a personal issue—it's an organizational one that affects productivity, innovation, and the bottom line.

lio & Gardner, 2005). By fostering authentic leadership, promoting psychological safety, and implementing practices reinforcing positive behaviors and mindsets, organizations can shift the momentum from a downward spiral to an upward one. This enhances individual well-being and team dynamics and contributes to a more resilient, innovative, and high-performing organizational culture.

The Roots of Negativity Bias

The impact of negativity bias in organizational contexts is profound and cannot be underestimated. As demonstrated by Kaplan et al. (2018) in their study of performance evaluations, negativity bias can significantly influence how leaders assess and respond to employee performance, potentially leading to skewed judgments and demotivating feedback. Furthermore, Corns (2018) provided an empirical examination of negativity bias, challenging some assumptions and highlighting the need for a more nuanced understanding of its role in different contexts. This body of research underscores the urgency of recognizing and actively addressing negativity bias in workplace settings, as it can profoundly impact employee morale, decision-making processes, and overall organizational culture.

> Negativity bias can quickly become the norm when left unaddressed, making it crucial to tackle issues head-on.

In the context of work, this negativity bias manifests in myriad ways. A single piece of constructive criticism can overshadow a glowing performance review. A minor disagreement with a colleague can color our entire perception of that relationship. A failed project from years ago can continue to haunt us, shaking our confidence and stifling our risk-taking.

As Mollie, a seasoned Chief People Officer, shared, "Even if there is an equal balance of positive and negative feedback, the negative components are more impactful and memorable." This imbalance can create a skewed perception of reality, where the challenges and frustrations of work take on outsized importance, overshadowing the many moments of progress, connection, and fulfillment.

To understand negativity bias in the workplace, we first need to recognize its deep roots in human psychology. For our early ancestors, the ability to quickly detect and respond to threats was a matter of life and death. Those more attuned to negative stimuli - the rustling in the bushes that could signal a predator, the slight change in a child's cry that could indicate illness - were more likely to survive and pass on their genes. As a result, our brains adapted to be more sensitive to negative information. We pay more attention to negative events, dwell on them longer, and give them more weight in our decision-making than equivalent positive ones. It's not that we don't notice or appreciate the good things—we do—but we're wired to be more impacted by the bad.

The foundational work of Rozin and Royzman (2001) on negativity bias provides a comprehensive framework for understanding this pervasive psychological phenomenon. Their research identified four fundamental principles that elucidate how and why negative stimuli significantly impact individuals more than positive ones of equal intensity. These principles offer valuable insights into the mechanisms underlying negativity bias and its implications for human behavior and cognition, particularly in organizational contexts.

The first principle, **negative potency**, posits that negative events or stimuli are more potent and salient than their positive counterparts. In the workplace, this might manifest as employees or leaders giving more weight to negative feedback or experiences than positive ones. For instance, a critical comment in a performance review might overshadow multiple positive remarks, potentially disproportionately impacting an employee's motivation and self-perception. Leaders must be aware of this tendency to ensure balanced and constructive feedback practices.

The second principle, steeper **negative gradients**, suggests that the negative impact of events increases more rapidly as they approach space or time compared to positive events. In an organizational setting, this could explain why impending challenges or potential problems often create more immediate stress and concern than approaching opportunities or rewards that generate excitement. This principle underscores the importance of effective change management and communication strategies, particularly when navigating organizational transitions or implementing new initiatives.

Negativity dominance, the third principle, refers to the tendency for negative elements to dominate when combining or integrating positive and negative entities. This principle has significant implications for decision-making processes in organizations. Interestingly, research suggests that a 3:1 ratio of positive to negative experiences or information feels balanced to the human brain, despite being objectively skewed toward positivity. This insight highlights how strongly negativity can impact our perceptions. For example, in evaluating a new project proposal, leaders or team members might give undue weight to potential risks or drawbacks, potentially overlooking substantial benefits. Without conscious effort, a proposal with three positive aspects and only one negative might be perceived as neutral or even slightly negative. Awareness of this bias can help develop more balanced assessment strategies, such as intentionally seeking out and emphasizing positive aspects to counteract the natural negative skew. This approach can foster a culture of innovative risk-taking by ensuring that opportunities are not unnecessarily dismissed due to an overemphasis on potential drawbacks.

The final principle, ***negative differentiation***, proposes that negative stimuli are more complex, differentiated, and elaborated than positive ones. In the workplace, this might manifest as employees or leaders spending more time and cognitive resources analyzing and discussing problems or conflicts than successes or positive developments. While thorough problem-solving is crucial, overanalyzing negative aspects can lead to a skewed focus and weight of importance on the challenges while minimizing what is going right.

Grasping the intricacies of these four principles equips leaders with a practical framework to tackle negativity bias in organizational settings. By understanding how negative potency, steeper gradients, dominance, and differentiation operate, leaders can devise targeted strategies to counterbalance these tendencies. This could involve implementing structured positive feedback mechanisms, consciously highlighting, and celebrating successes, or training employees in cognitive reframing techniques. This knowledge can also guide the design of organizational processes and communication strategies that acknowledge the natural human tendency towards negativity bias, fostering a more balanced and positive workplace culture.

Rozin and Royzman's work not only illuminates the mechanisms of negativity bias but also underscores its pervasive nature across various domains of human experience. In organizational contexts, this pervasiveness underscores the need for ongoing, systemic efforts to address negativity bias, rather than viewing it as a one-time challenge. By integrating an understanding of these principles into leadership development, organizational design, and culture-building initiatives, companies can work towards creating environments that acknowledge the reality of negativity bias while actively cultivating positivity and resilience over the long term.

Building on this foundation, Vaish, Grossmann, and Woodward (2008) reviewed developmental research, demonstrating that negativity bias emerges early in life and plays a significant role in social-emotional development. Their findings suggest that this bias is not merely a learned response but a fundamental aspect of human psychology that shapes our perceptions and interactions from infancy onward. Complementing these insights, Baumeister et al. (2001) presented compelling evidence for the "bad is stronger than good" phenomenon across various domains of psychological research, including relationships, emotions, learning, and information processing.

In the case of a new employee transitioning from a toxic work environment to a healthier one, their previous negative experiences can significantly color their perceptions and interactions in the new organization, even in the face of a more positive culture. For instance, if the employee experienced frequent criticism or lack of recognition in their previous job, they might be hypersensitive to any feedback in the unfamiliar environment, interpreting constructive comments as harsh criticism. This negativity bias can lead to a prolonged period of guardedness and skepticism, making it challenging for the manager to build rapport, trust, and respect. Research suggests that it may take approximately five positive interactions to counterbalance the impact of a single negative one (Gottman, 1994). In this scenario, the new employee might require numerous positive experiences - such as supportive team interactions, successful project completions, or instances of managerial praise - before they begin to overcome their ingrained negative expectations. This process could extend the time needed for full integration into the new culture from a few months to a year or more, depending on the severity of the previous toxic environment and the individual's resilience. The manager needs to be patient, consistent, and intentional in fostering positive interactions and providing clear, supportive communication to gradually reshape the employee's perceptions and build a foundation of trust in the new, healthier work culture.

> For every negative interaction, it takes approximately five positive ones to counterbalance its impact.

The COVID-19 pandemic has only amplified this dynamic. With the sudden shift to remote work, the blurring of work-life boundaries, and the pervasive sense of uncertainty and stress, many employees have found themselves struggling with heightened anxiety, burnout, and negativity. As Mel, a healthcare executive, put it, "As a global society, we focus on the things that are not working. The great resignation, the quiet quitting, now the quiet vacationing." In this context, it's a priority more than ever for leaders to recognize the power of negativity bias and take proactive steps to counteract it. But what exactly does that look like in practice? To answer that question, let's dive into some specific ways negativity bias manifests in the workplace.

Negativity bias can rear its head in countless ways, often subtly shaping the tone and dynamics of workplace interactions. Here are a few of the most common manifestations, as described by the executives I interviewed:

Rumors and Gossip: When there's a vacuum of information, negativity bias can fuel the rumor mill, as employees speculate about potential downsizings, leadership changes, or other perceived threats. Mel noted that negative gossip "can go viral if there isn't a way to help see an alternative opinion."

Resistance to Change: Negativity bias can make employees more prone to see the potential downsides of any change rather than the opportunities. As Erica shared, people may resist innovation because "they're afraid of being in trouble or afraid to make mistakes."

Assuming the Worst: When an email goes unanswered, or a meeting gets rescheduled, negativity bias can lead employees to assume the worst rather than giving their colleagues the benefit of the doubt. This can quickly sour working relationships and erode trust.

Dwelling on Failures: A single setback or failure can loom large in employees' minds, overshadowing a long record of accomplishment of successes. As Peter put it, "When someone makes a mistake that everyone knows about, what they really want is for it to be acknowledged and a promise to improve."

Complaining and Venting: Negativity can be contagious as employees bond over shared frustrations and complaints. While some venting is natural and even healthy, a culture of chronic complaining can quickly take root and drag down morale.

These manifestations may seem small in isolation, but over time, they can negatively affect the overall workplace climate. As negativity becomes the default lens through which employees view their work and each other, it can create a self-perpetuating cycle that is difficult to break.

Darin, a construction executive, described this dynamic vividly: "If you don't address negativity, it grows and spreads. Eventually, it becomes the norm. New employees and younger staff join the company and assume this negative atmosphere is just how things are supposed to be." Negativity can become ingrained in the very culture of an organization, passed down from one generation of employees to the next.

So, what are the tangible impacts of this negativity on individuals, teams, and the organization? Let's take a closer look.

The Toll of Negativity on Employee Well-Being

One of the most immediate and visceral consequences of negativity bias is the toll it takes on employee mental health and well-being. When every day brings a barrage of negative interactions, stressful challenges, and perceived slights, it can quickly wear down even the most resilient individuals. Carolyn, a project executive in the construction industry, shared a poignant example of how negativity impacted her well-being: "The negativity was so overwhelming, it limited my ability to contribute. The stress was so intense that I couldn't even find the time to perform at my best." The constant strain of negativity left her depleted and unable to bring her whole self to work.

Many of the executives I spoke with echoed this sentiment. They described employees who were visibly stressed, anxious, and disengaged—not because they didn't care about their work but because they were buckling under the weight of a negative environment.

Aaron, a healthcare CEO, put it this way: "My goal is for all our team members to feel fulfilled, both in their work and personal lives. If someone isn't in the right role or even the right career, I want them to find a path that truly makes them happy." This speaks to a fundamental truth: when negativity undermines employees' sense of well-being and fulfillment, it's not just a personal issue—it's an organizational one.

The business costs of this negativity-induced burnout are significant. Stressed, unhappy employees are more likely to take sick days, make mistakes, and leave the organization altogether. As Dan noted, "When negativity goes unchecked, it has a real impact on the organization. We've seen that it significantly slows down our ability to achieve our goals." In other words, negativity doesn't just hurt people - it hurts productivity.

However, the impacts of negativity go beyond individual well-being and performance. It can also corrosively affect entire teams and their ability to work together effectively.

The Erosion of Team Trust and Collaboration

Negativity bias thrives in an environment of distrust and disconnection. When employees quickly assume the worst about each other's intentions or competence, building positive, collaborative relationships essential for team success can take much work.

Carolyn shared a vivid example of how negativity can poison a team dynamic: "Without trust, I don't respect. Without respect, it breaks the whole relationship." In this case, a lack of trust between two team members had escalated into a complete communication breakdown, derailing projects, and creating a toxic atmosphere for everyone around them.

This erosion of trust can also make it difficult for teams to take risks, think creatively, and push past challenges. As Erica described, "When there's a lack of trust, people tend to isolate themselves. They avoid collaboration, sometimes even resort to dishonesty, and stop being innovative. They're afraid to take risks or try new ideas because they fear getting into trouble or making mistakes." Negativity creates a climate of fear and self-preservation, where employees are more focused on avoiding blame or conflict than on working together towards shared goals. This can stifle the kind of open communication, healthy debate, and creative problem-solving that are the lifeblood of high-performing teams.

Mel summed it up nicely: "It can go viral if there isn't a way to help see an alternative opinion." When negativity takes hold, it can quickly spread throughout a team, creating an echo chamber of cynicism and discontent. Breaking out of that cycle requires a concerted effort to inject positivity, build trust, and create space for diverse perspectives—a task that falls squarely on the shoulders of leaders.

The Leadership Challenge of a Negative Culture

> Leaders must recognize that they are not immune to negativity bias and actively work to counteract it in themselves and their teams.

For leaders, negativity bias presents a uniquely thorny challenge. On the one hand, they are not immune to its effects - they, too, can fall into the trap of dwelling on problems, assuming the worst, or getting defensive in the face of criticism. On the other hand, they are uniquely positioned to set the tone for their organizations and drive positive change. Many executives I spoke with described their journey of recognizing and overcoming negative biases. Heather, a Chief People Officer (CPO) in the construction industry, shared, "When I realized this in my mid-twenties, it completely transformed my approach to leading teams." Becoming aware of her tendency to focus on the negative was a transformative moment in her leadership development, but awareness is just the first step.

Leaders must also take purposeful action to counteract negativity and cultivate a more positive culture. This starts with modeling the right behaviors and attitudes. As Darin put it, "Leading by example is essential. Without it, your other efforts are likely wasted. But even when you do lead by example, you must reinforce it with words, constantly communicating and emphasizing your message." Leaders must walk the talk - demonstrating positivity, resilience, and trust in their actions and communications. They must be willing to acknowledge and own their mistakes, as Peter noted: "When a person screws up, and everybody knows they screw up, what they're craving is an acknowledgment and a commitment to do better."

Most importantly, leaders must be proactive in addressing negativity head-on. As Peter warned, "Ignoring people's problems teaches them not to come to you. The issues don't go away - they grow silently. You end up in the dark because your team learns either you don't care or you're not helpful." Negativity is not a problem that will solve itself. Left unchecked, it will only grow and spread, undermining the very foundation of the organization. Leaders must be willing to confront it directly, with empathy and skill.

Brain Work - Neuroscience and Leadership - The Marvel of Plasticity

From a psychologist's perspective, understanding the neuroscience of negativity in the workplace is crucial for fostering healthy, productive organizational cultures. The human brain, a marvel of pliability, is exquisitely attuned to its environment, constantly scanning for threats and opportunities. In the work context, this ancient survival mechanism can sometimes work against us, creating a cascade of negative effects that ripple through entire organizations.

At the heart of this phenomenon lies negativity bias, a well-documented tendency of our brains to give more weight to negative experiences than positive ones. While once crucial for survival, this bias can lead to a disproportionate focus on workplace problems, conflicts, and challenges. As a result, employees may experience heightened stress responses, decreased job satisfaction, and lower productivity. The impact of this bias is so potent that, as Baumeister and colleagues (2001) found, negative events exert a more substantial influence on individuals than positive events of equal intensity.

> The human brain is wired to give greater weight to negative experiences, but we can rewire it through intentional positive practices.

Compounding this issue is the presence of mirror neurons in our brains. These remarkable cells fire not only when we act but also when we observe others performing the same action. This neural mirroring extends to emotions, facilitating what psychologists call emotional contagion. Negative emotions can spread rapidly in a workplace, infecting team dynamics and organizational culture. Barsade's (2002) research vividly demonstrated how a single team member's mood could influence the entire group's emotional state and behavior.

However, the brain's plasticity offers a ray of hope. Neuroplasticity, the brain's ability to form new neural connections throughout life, suggests that we can actively reshape our cognitive and emotional patterns. Davidson and Begley's (2012) work on neuroplasticity indicates that intentional practices, such as mindfulness and positive attunement, can shift our emotional set points over time. Emotional set points refer to the average level of positive and negative emotions that a person experiences. This insight opens possibilities for interventions to help individuals and organizations cultivate more positive, resilient mindsets.

The physiological impact of workplace negativity is equally significant. Chronic exposure to negative work environments can lead to elevated levels of stress hormones, particularly cortisol. McEwen's (1998) research on allostatic load illuminates the cumulative toll that chronic stress takes on the brain and body. Prolonged cortisol exposure can damage the hippocampus, a brain region crucial for memory and learning, and suppress the immune system, increasing vulnerability to burnout and illness.

One of the most striking findings in recent years is the neurological overlap between social and physical pain. Eisenberger et al. (2003) used fMRI studies to demonstrate that social pain, such as that caused by workplace rejection or conflict, activates the same brain regions as physical pain. This finding underscores negative social interactions' genuine, tangible impact on an individual's well-being, fostering a sense of empathy and understanding in the audience.

Given these insights, psychologists and organizational experts have developed strategies to counteract workplace negativity. These include promoting psychological safety, a term coined by Edmondson (1999), which refers to a climate where people feel safe to express their thoughts and feelings without fear of negative consequences. Implementing regular stress-reduction practices and fostering emotional intelligence among team members and leaders are also key strategies.

The role of leadership in shaping organizational emotional climate cannot be overstated. Goleman et al. (2001) found that a leader's mood and behaviors can drive up to 30% of a company's emotional climate. This underscores the importance of developing emotionally intelligent, empathetic leaders who can create a buffer against negativity and model positive behaviors.

The economic impact of workplace negativity is staggering, with estimates suggesting that disengagement and stress cost U.S. industries hundreds of billions of dollars annually. This stark reality should motivate us to understand and apply these neuroscientific insights. By doing so, organizations have the potential to create more positive, productive, and fulfilling work environments. As psychologists, our role is to bridge the gap between this cutting-edge neuroscience and practical, implementable strategies that can transform workplace cultures, one brain at a time. For leaders, transformation begins with facilitating crucial conversations to raise awareness about negativity within the workplace.

Conclusion

The nature and impact of negativity bias in the workplace are clear. It is a pervasive and insidious force that can sap the energy, creativity, and productivity of individuals and teams. It can turn the workplace into a battleground of cynicism, distrust, and discontent. Left unchecked, it can drive away top talent and undermine the success of the organization.

However, the executives I interviewed clarified that negativity is not an insurmountable challenge. With awareness, intentionality, and skill, leaders can learn to recognize and counter the effects of negativity bias. They can model positivity, build trust, and create a culture where employees feel safe to take risks, voice concerns, and work together towards shared goals.

This process takes time and effort. It requires ongoing effort, resilience, and a willingness to confront uncomfortable truths. But the payoff—a workplace where people feel valued, engaged, and inspired to do their best—is more than worth it.

In the following chapters, we'll explore the specific strategies and practices these executives have used to combat negativity and cultivate a more positive culture. We'll also explore the power of effective communication, the importance of building psychological safety, and the role of authentic servant leadership in driving change. But for now, the message is simple: negativity bias is real, and it's hurting our organizations. It's up to us as leaders to face it with courage and compassion. When we do, we open the door to a workplace that isn't just productive but truly thriving—a place where people can bring their full selves, take pride in their work, and find a sense of meaning and belonging.

That's the vision that drives me, and I hope it will inspire you as you read on. Together, we can learn to spiral up, countering the pull of negativity with the upward momentum of positivity, growth, and change. It won't be easy, but it will be worth it. Let's get started.

Recap: The Nature and Impact of Negativity Bias

This chapter explored the pervasive challenge of negativity bias in the workplace, its roots in human psychology, and its far-reaching impacts on individuals, teams, and organizations.

Key Insights:

* Negativity bias is a survival mechanism that gives greater weight to negative experiences than positive ones.
* In the workplace, negativity bias can erode trust, stifle innovation, and undermine leadership efforts.
* Negative spirals can create self-perpetuating cycles of decreased motivation, productivity, and deteriorating relationships.
* Manifestations of negativity bias include rumors, resistance to change, assuming the worst, dwelling on failures, and chronic complaining.
* Negativity takes a significant toll on employee well-being, team trust, collaboration, and overall organizational performance.
* Leaders play a crucial role in recognizing and actively addressing negativity bias to foster a positive workplace culture.

5 Leadership Reflection Questions:

1. How have I observed negativity bias manifesting in my team or organization? What specific examples come to mind?

2. In what ways might my own negativity bias be influencing my leadership decisions or interactions with team members?

3. How effective have I been in addressing and countering negativity in my workplace? What strategies have worked well, and where have I fallen short?

4. How can I better model positivity and resilience for my team, especially during challenging times?

5. What steps can I take to create a culture of psychological safety where team members feel comfortable voicing concerns without fear of negative repercussions?

Team Discussion Exercise: Negativity Bias Awareness

<u>Objective</u>: To increase awareness of negativity bias and its impact on team dynamics and decision-making.

<u>Instructions</u>:

1. Divide the team into small groups of 3-4 people.

2. Ask each group to recall a recent team project or initiative and list:
    a) Three challenges or setbacks they encountered
    b) Three successes or positive outcomes

3. Have groups discuss:
    - Which list was easier to generate and why?
    - How much time and energy did the team spend focusing on each category during the project?
    - How did the focus on negatives vs. positives impact team morale and performance?

4. Assemble the team to share insights from their group discussions.

5. As a team, brainstorm strategies for:
    - Balancing attention to problems with recognition of successes
    - Reframing negative situations to find opportunities for growth or learning
    - Cultivating a more positive team culture while still addressing challenges effectively

6. Conclude by having each team member share one action they'll take to counter negativity bias in their work moving forward.

This exercise helps teams recognize how negativity bias operates in their own context and encourages proactive steps to create a more balanced, positive work environment.

Chapter 2
The Role of Leadership in Shaping Workplace Culture

As we delve deeper into the complex dynamics of negativity bias-a psychological phenomenon where humans pay more attention to and give more weight to negative experiences and emotions than positive ones-in the workplace, one thing becomes abundantly clear: leadership plays a pivotal role in amplifying or mitigating its effects. The attitudes, behaviors, and practices of those at the helm profoundly influence the overall organizational climate. In this chapter, we'll explore the link between leadership and workplace culture, drawing on organizational psychology insights and the executives' real-world experiences I interviewed. We'll examine how different leadership styles, such as autocratic, transformational, and servant leadership approaches, that can fuel negativity or create the conditions for positivity and resilience to thrive.

At the heart of our discussion lies the transformative power of authentic leadership - a theory that underscores the significance of self-awareness, transparency, and ethical behavior in driving positive organizational outcomes. We'll delve into how authentic leaders can embody the vulnerability, empathy, and growth mindset that are crucial for overcoming negativity bias, inspiring a new era of workplace culture.

Another key aspect we'll explore is the concept of psychological capital - a potent blend of self-efficacy, optimism, hope, and resilience. This invaluable resource equips individuals and teams to bounce back from setbacks and maintain a positive outlook in the face of challenges. We'll delve into how leaders can foster this resilience and optimism within their organizations, creating a robust defense against the corrosive effects of negativity.

> Authentic leadership builds trust through consistent alignment between words and actions, transparency, and genuine care for employees.

Throughout the chapter, we'll ground these concepts in the lived experiences of the executives I spoke with, sharing their stories of struggle and triumph in the battle against workplace negativity. For instance, we'll discuss how a CEO in the tech industry transformed a toxic work environment into a thriving one by implementing authentic leadership practices. Their insights offer a roadmap for leaders looking to shape a more positive, productive, and resilient culture - one conversation, one decision, and one interaction at a time.

The Leadership-Culture Connection

To understand the role of leadership in addressing workplace negativity, we first need to recognize the inextricable link between leadership and organizational culture. Workplace culture, in the words of renowned management scholar Edgar Schein, is 'a pattern of shared basic assumptions that the group learned as it solved its problems of external adaptation and internal integration, that has worked well enough to be considered valid and, therefore, to be taught to new members as the correct way to perceive, think, and feel about those problems.' In simpler terms, workplace culture is the collective beliefs, values, and behaviors that shape how work is done in an organization.

Culture is the unwritten rules, shared beliefs, and behaviors shaping how things get done in an organization. While a multitude of factors influence culture—from industry and market conditions to employees' individual personalities—leadership is the most potent force in shaping it. As Dan, a non-profit CEO, said, "The worst behavior sets the culture of an organization the leader is willing to tolerate." What leaders choose to pay attention to, prioritize, reward, or punish sends a powerful signal about what is truly valued and expected within the organization.

When leaders consistently demonstrate integrity, respect, and a commitment to employee well-being, the tone ripples throughout the organization. Conversely, when leaders disregard toxic behavior-which can include bullying, harassment, discrimination, or any other behavior that undermines the well-being of individuals or the organization as a whole-prioritize short-term results over long-term sustainability, or fail to model their values, it can create a culture of cynicism, fear, and negativity.

> The worst behavior a leader tolerates sets the culture of an organization.

A construction Chief Operations Officer, Darin provided a vivid example of leadership's impact on culture. He said, "Our culture reflected old-school instruction. I joined the company when it bordered on dictatorial leadership." This authoritarian style had taken root in the organization. It created a culture of compliance and fear, which resulted in reduced innovation and engagement. Changing this dynamic demanded a leadership overhaul. The new approach needed to focus on empowerment, collaboration, and trust.

The old-school dictatorial style created a need for more effective leadership. This led to the concept of authentic leadership. Researchers Bruce Avolio and Fred Luthans defined authentic leaders. These leaders are deeply self-aware. They understand how they think and behave. Others see them as aware of values, morals, knowledge, and strengths. They know their operational context well. They are confident, hopeful, optimistic, and resilient. They also possess high moral character. In essence, authentic leaders have integrity. They practice what they preach. They lead with deep conviction and consistency. Studies show this leadership style creates positive, engaged, resilient workplace cultures.

The Power of Authentic Leadership

So, what does authentic leadership look like in practice, and how can it help to combat negativity bias in the workplace? The executives I spoke with offered a wealth of insights and examples. Mollie, from the financial sector, emphasized the importance of vulnerability and transparency in authentic leadership: "It's crucial to be vulnerable and transparent. As female executives, we're often told to hide our emotions at work. I believe that's the wrong approach." Authentic leaders are willing to show up as their whole, flawed human selves. They don't try to project an image of invincibility or perfection but acknowledge their struggles, doubts, and mistakes. This vulnerability can profoundly disarm, breaking down barriers and creating a space for genuine connection and trust.

Mel, a senior living executive, described how this plays out in her leadership practice: "It begins with how we speak, and then it's reflected in our actions. When I'm curious, I ask more questions. This curiosity shows in both my words and my behavior."

By modeling curiosity, empathy, and a willingness to learn, authentic leaders create an environment where others can do the same. They foster a culture of psychological safety, where employees feel empowered to speak up, challenge the status quo, and take risks without fear of retribution.

This is particularly important in the context of addressing negativity bias. When employees feel heard, respected, and valued, they are far less likely to fall into cynicism, blame, or disengagement patterns. They are more likely to approach challenges with a growth mindset, seeing obstacles as opportunities for learning and improvement rather than threats to be avoided. Peter, an education CEO, summed it up this way: "Colin Powell said it's a bad sign if people stop bringing you their problems. It means they've either decided you can't help, or that you don't care, and both are issues for a leader."

Authentic leaders understand that building trust and psychological safety is an ongoing process requiring consistent attention and effort. They seek out and listen to employee concerns, even (and especially) when those concerns are difficult or uncomfortable to hear. Erica, an executive director in the education sector, shared how she puts this into practice: "I purposely observed the meetings and brought the two of them together to give feedback to each other. I didn't want them to think I had all the answers, but encouraged them to come up with solutions together." By creating spaces for open dialogue, constructive feedback, and collaborative problem-solving, authentic leaders demonstrate their commitment to employee voice and agency. They show they value the result and the process of getting together.

Of course, this can be a challenging process. Authentic leadership requires a willingness to confront brutal truths, to have uncomfortable conversations, and to make tough decisions. It demands emotional intelligence and self-regulation, allowing leaders to remain grounded and centered even in the face of stress, adversity, or criticism. This is where the concept of psychological capital comes into play. Leaders high in psychological capital - that combination of self-efficacy, optimism, hope, and resilience - are better equipped to navigate the challenges of authentic leadership. They have the inner resources and strength to remain true to their values, even when going is tough.

> Psychological safety is not just a 'nice-to-have'—it's essential for innovation, engagement, and organizational success.

Cultivating Psychological Capital

So, how can leaders build and leverage psychological capital, both within themselves and their teams? The executives I spoke with offered a range of strategies and practices. Aaron, a CEO, highlighted the importance of focusing on strengths and values. He uses a "people analyzer" from the Entrepreneur Operating System's traction model: once a year, employees are evaluated based on core values. By regularly assessing and affirming each team member's unique strengths and contributions, leaders help build a sense of self-efficacy and worth. They counteract the natural tendency toward negativity bias by shining a light on what's working, what's good, and what's possible. Heather, CPO, described how her organization prioritizes gratitude as a way of building psychological capital: "We have these leadership huddles with people from all over the organization, and it starts with people submitting what they're grateful for or how they want to celebrate somebody else."

> Cultivating psychological capital (hope, efficacy, resilience, optimism) equips teams to navigate challenges and thrive.

A simple practice of regularly expressing appreciation and celebrating wins, however small, can have a profound impact on a team's overall emotional climate. It helps offset the brain's negativity bias by training attention on the positive, building a reservoir of goodwill and resilience. Of course, cultivating psychological capital isn't about focusing on the positive. It's also about developing the skills and mindset to navigate challenges and setbacks effectively. Jeff, a non-profit CEO, spoke about the importance of framing problems as opportunities for growth and learning: "Every problem that we encounter is an opportunity for us to learn, grow, and improve." By modeling this growth mindset, leaders help their teams approach obstacles with curiosity and creativity rather than fear or avoidance. They foster a culture of experimentation and innovation, where failure is seen as a necessary part of the learning process rather than a mark of inadequacy.

Underpinning these practices is a belief in people's potential and resilience. Authentic leaders with high psychological capital deeply trust their own and others' ability to rise to the occasion, find solutions, and bounce back from adversity. They communicate this belief through words and actions, creating a self-fulfilling cycle of positivity and growth.

Moving From Theory to Practice

Knowing about authentic leadership and psychological capital in theory is one thing; putting it into practice in the face of real-world challenges and pressures is another. The executives I spoke with were candid about the difficulties and pitfalls of leading authentically in a world that often rewards quick fixes, short-term thinking, and a "win at all costs" mentality. Carolyn provides insights from the construction industry, describing the toll that this pressure can take: "I was so overwhelmed and restricted that I couldn't give my best. The stress left me with no time to perform as I desired." I dare say, even the most well-intentioned leaders can fall prey to negativity bias and burnout if they don't prioritize their well-being and resilience. Authentic leadership requires a commitment to self-care, setting boundaries, and modeling the kind of work-life integration that allows for long-term sustainability.

It also requires a willingness to have difficult conversations and make unpopular decisions for a higher purpose. Mollie spoke about balancing empathy with accountability: "As a leader, I need to stay connected to the organization's purpose and represent it, but I must do it in a way that shows I care for and support my team." Authentic leaders understand that there will be times when they need to push their teams out of their comfort zones, challenge long-held assumptions, or make tough calls in the face of resistance. The key is to do so from a place of genuine care and respect, always keeping the organization's long-term well-being and its people at the forefront.

Authentic leadership and the cultivation of psychological capital are journeys, not destinations. They require ongoing self-reflection, humility, and a commitment to growth and learning. They demand a willingness to sit with discomfort, lean into vulnerability, and trust in the resilience of oneself and others. However, as the stories and examples shared by the executives in this chapter demonstrate, the payoff of this work is immense. By modeling authenticity, fostering psychological safety, and building resilience, leaders have the power to shape workplace cultures that bring out the best in people - cultures where negativity is met with empathy and understanding, where challenges are seen as opportunities, and where every individual feels valued, supported, and empowered to thrive.

Codifying the Competencies: A Case for Self-Leadership

The intricate connection between leadership and organizational culture has been the subject of extensive research and discussion in management literature. As we transition from examining the Leadership-Culture Connection, the Power of Authentic Leadership, and the importance of Cultivating Psychological Capital, we delve deeper into the essential competencies that leaders must possess to shape and transform organizational culture effectively. This section explores the qualitative research method findings utilizing Charmaz's (2014) grounded theory codification process, which revealed eight essential leadership competencies for driving cultural change.

The grounded theory approach provides a systematic method for analyzing qualitative data and deriving theoretical insights. Through this process, researchers can identify patterns, themes, and relationships within the data, developing a coherent theoretical framework. In this study, the codification process uncovered a set of higher-level and lower-level categories that represent essential leadership traits and sub-traits necessary for cultural transformation.

The findings emphasize a crucial insight: the leader within must be cultivated before any cultural change initiative can be fully executed. The success of transforming organizational culture is intrinsically linked to the maturity and personal growth of the leader guiding the process. This revelation underscores the importance of self-leadership disciplines and continuous professional development for those in leadership positions.

Based on extensive literary research and in-depth interviews with seasoned executive leaders, eight core competencies emerged as critical for effective organizational change. These competencies highlight the priority of professional responsibility in self-leadership disciplines and development. Let's explore these soft skills and competencies:

> **1. Leadership Practices**: Effective leaders must adopt modern approaches that align with contemporary workplace dynamics. This involves providing constructive feedback, aligning behavior with organizational values, and setting clear expectations. One executive (Darin) noted, "As leaders, we must walk the talk. Our actions and attitudes set the tone for the entire organization. When we consistently demonstrate the positive behaviors and mindset we want to see, it creates a ripple effect throughout the workplace culture."
>
> **2. Communication**: Open and transparent communication addresses negativity and fosters a positive culture. This includes promoting open dialogue, modeling positive communication, and

encouraging diverse viewpoints. Mollie emphasized, "Listening openly to understand root causes is essential when addressing workplace negativity."

3. Respect and Trust: Building a culture of respect and trust is fundamental to organizational success. Leaders must focus on respecting employees as individuals and fostering collaboration. As one leader, Erica, said, "Building meaningful, trusting relationships beyond superficialities is key to overcoming negativity."

4. Problem-Solving: Proactive problem-solving is essential for addressing issues before they escalate. This involves acknowledging problems, addressing them promptly, and engaging with negativity to understand its underlying causes. An executive (Peter) shared, "Recognizing the consequences of disengagement, such as lost productivity and revenue, is crucial for effective problem-solving."

5. Employee Well-Being: Prioritizing employee well-being is key for combating negativity and fostering a positive culture. This includes focusing on employee well-being, recognizing team contributions, and leveraging individual talents. Mel noted, "Showing compassion for employees as people is vital for creating a supportive environment."

6. Innovation and Growth: Leaders must create an environment encouraging innovation and supporting growth. This involves addressing fear, providing necessary resources, and fostering a culture of psychological safety. An interviewee (Peter) emphasized, "Encouraging innovation and learning from failure is essential for organizational growth."

7. Organizational Culture: Shaping a positive culture requires leaders to address negativity promptly and align behavior with values. As one executive (Darin) stated, "Negativity can quickly become the norm when left unaddressed, making it crucial to tackle issues head-on."

8. Relationships: Building solid and authentic relationships is fundamental to addressing negativity and fostering a positive culture. This includes trust-building, fostering collaboration, and recognizing team contributions. "Caring and compassionate relationships are key to reducing negativity in the workplace" (Mel).

These eight competencies represent an integrated approach to leadership development and cultural transformation. They emphasize the importance of self-awareness, emotional intelligence, and interpersonal skills in driving organizational change. By focusing on these competencies, leaders can create a positive work environment that fosters engagement, innovation, and productivity. The significance of these eight competencies lies in their interconnectedness and role in shaping organizational culture. They provide a comprehensive framework for leaders to assess their strengths and areas for improvement, guiding their personal and professional development. This interconnectedness underscores the complexity and depth of the leadership role in cultural change, ensuring that leaders possess the necessary skills and mindset to navigate the complexities of organizational transformation.

It is important to note that developing these competencies is an ongoing process. Carolyn said, "Promoting positivity through messaging and gratitude can help shift the cultural tide, but it requires consistent effort and commitment." This highlights the need for continuous learning and growth for leaders, reinforcing the idea that leadership is a journey of continuous improvement.

A Look in Mirror Before Pointing the Finger

The critical insight that successful cultural transformation requires more than just implementing steps or strategies. It demands an integrated and comprehensive approach to leadership development. The leader who grows within is better equipped to guide organizational change effectively. As such, it's an invitation for leaders to look in the mirror first before pointing the finger at what needs to change in their organization.

The journey of cultural transformation begins with self-reflection and personal growth. By developing these eight core competencies, leaders can cultivate the internal resources necessary to navigate the challenges of organizational change.

This introspective approach not only enhances the leader's effectiveness but also sets a powerful example for others in the organization to follow, emphasizing the necessity of these qualities in a leader.

The success of any cultural change initiative hinges on the leader's ability to embody the desired values and behaviors. As Aaron eloquently stated, "Culture change starts with the leader. It's about walking the talk and demonstrating the values we want to see in our organization." This profound insight reminds us that true cultural transformation is an inside-out process, beginning with the leader's own growth and development. Leaders must not only possess these competencies but also model them in their daily interactions and decision-making, thereby reinforcing their importance and encouraging their adoption throughout the organization. In embracing this integrated approach to leadership and cultural change, organizations can create environments that weather the storms of negativity and thrive in the face of challenges. By prioritizing the development of these essential leadership competencies, leaders can unlock the full potential of their teams and drive lasting, positive change in their organizations.

> Leaders must balance authenticity with adaptability, personal values with organizational needs.

Conclusion

As we've seen throughout this chapter, the role of leadership in shaping workplace culture and addressing negativity bias cannot be overstated. The attitudes, behaviors, and practices of those in positions of power send a powerful signal about what is expected and valued within an organization. When leaders embody the principles of authentic leadership - self-awareness, transparency, ethical behavior, and a commitment to employee well-being - they create the conditions for positivity and resilience to flourish. By modeling vulnerability, empathy, and a growth mindset, they give others permission and encouragement to do the same. Furthermore, by actively cultivating psychological capital - that invaluable combination of self-efficacy, optimism, hope, and resilience - leaders equip themselves and their teams with the inner resources to navigate even the toughest challenges. They build trust, goodwill, and mutual respect that can weather any storm. But as the executives' stories also remind us, this work is not for the faint of heart.

Authentic leadership requires courage, self-reflection, and commitment that goes beyond the usual platitudes of management theory. It demands a willingness to confront hard truths, have uncomfortable conversations, and make decisions prioritizing long-term, collective well-being over short-term, individual gain. It's a journey that requires ongoing practice, humility, and a deep belief in people's potential to learn, grow, and thrive together. It's not about being perfect but about being perfectly human and creating space for others to do the same.

As we explore overcoming negativity bias in the workplace, the insights and examples shared in this chapter offer a guiding light. They remind us that change is possible, that culture is malleable, and that each of us has a role in shaping the environments in which we work and live. By embracing the principles of authentic leadership and actively building our own and others' psychological capital, we can begin to spiral up—to create workplaces that bring out the best in people and harness the power of positivity and potential. It's a vision worth striving for that starts with each of us leading from a place of authenticity, courage, and heart.

Recap: The Role of Leadership in Shaping Workplace Culture

This chapter explored the strategic role of leadership in influencing workplace culture, particularly in addressing negativity bias and fostering a positive environment.

Key Insights:

* Leadership is the most potent force in shaping organizational culture.
* Authentic leadership, characterized by self-awareness, transparency, and ethical behavior, is crucial for creating positive workplace cultures.
* Psychological capital (self-efficacy, optimism, hope, and resilience) equips leaders and teams to overcome negativity bias.

* Vulnerability and transparency in leadership can break down barriers and create trust.
* Cultivating psychological safety is essential for encouraging open dialogue and innovation.
* Eight core leadership competencies were identified as critical for driving cultural change, including effective communication, respect and trust-building, and prioritizing employee well-being.
* Cultural transformation begins with the leader's own growth and development.

5 Leadership Reflection Questions:

1. How do my leadership practices currently contribute to or mitigate negativity in my organization?

2. In what ways can I demonstrate more vulnerability and transparency as a leader to build trust with my team?

3. How am I actively cultivating psychological capital (self-efficacy, optimism, hope, and resilience) in myself and my team?

4. Which of the eight core leadership competencies do I need to develop further to drive positive cultural change?

5. How can I better model the behaviors and values I want to see in my organization's culture?

Team Exercise: The Leadership Vacuum

Objective: To show the strategic role of leadership in team dynamics and the potential consequences when leadership is absent.

Materials: A complex puzzle or building set (e.g., Lego set), blindfolds, timer

Time: 30-40 minutes

Instructions:

1. Divide participants into teams of 5-6 people.

2. Assign one person in each team as the leader.

3. Give each team an identical complex puzzle or building set.

4. Explain the rules:

    - The goal is to complete the puzzle/structure within 15 minutes.

    - Only the leader can see the instructions.

    - Other team members are blindfolded and can only follow verbal instructions from the leader.

    - The leader cannot touch the pieces or physically help.

5. Allow teams to work for 5 minutes with their leaders guiding them.

6. After 5 minutes, announce that all leaders must step away and remain silent for the next 5 minutes, simulating an absence of leadership.

7. After this period, allow leaders to return for the final 5 minutes.

8. Once time is up, have teams remove blindfolds and discuss their experiences.

Debrief Discussion:
1. How did the team function when the leader was present? What worked well?

2. What challenges arose when the leader stepped away? How did team dynamics change?

3. How did it feel to be a team member without clear direction?

4. For leaders: What was it like to watch your team struggle without being able to intervene?

5. What strategies did teams develop to cope with the absence of leadership?

6. How does this exercise relate to real-world situations in your organization?

7. What lessons can we draw about the importance of consistent, effective leadership?

8. How can teams build resilience to function effectively even when leadership is temporarily absent?

This exercise vividly shows the role of leadership in providing direction, coordination, and support. It also highlights the potential challenges and adaptations that occur when leadership is suddenly removed. The experience can lead to valuable insights about the importance of clear communication, team resilience, and the impact of leadership on team performance and morale.

PART 2: The SPIRAL 6-Step Framework for Transforming Negativity

Chapter 3

Step 1 - Strengthen Authentic Leadership

Your Best Boss

OUR JOURNEY TOWARD TRANSFORMATIVE organizational change begins with a profound exploration of leadership. For the past decade, I have been facilitating a four-day leadership training program. We kick off the program with a powerful exercise, the 'Best Boss' reflection. This exercise is not just a starting point, but a cornerstone that sets the tone for our journey and helps us understand the essence of authentic leadership. The 'Best Boss' reflection is a crucial and transformative starting point for our journey towards intentional leadership. Imagine a room full of aspiring leaders with unique experiences and perspectives. As the facilitator, I invite participants to reflect on their career journeys and recall the boss who made the most significant positive impact on their professional lives. The room buzzes with energy as stories are shared, memories rekindled, and insights gained. This exercise, the 'Best Boss' reflection, is a powerful tool in strengthening authentic leadership.

"Take a moment to think about your best boss," I prompt. "What qualities did they possess? How did they support your growth and development? In what ways did they advocate for your success?" As participants engage in lively discussions, a common thread emerges. The characteristics of these exemplary leaders paint a vivid picture of authentic, empowering leadership. Words like 'encouraging,' 'supportive,' 'proactive,' 'empathetic,' 'compassionate,' 'capable,' 'trustworthy,' 'consistent,' 'available,' and 'advocate' fill the whiteboard. These qualities resonate deeply, reminding us of a great leader's profound impact on individual careers and organizations, instilling hope, and optimism for the future.

To contrast and deepen our understanding, we then create a comparison list of "worst bosses." Circling back to the introduction, Robert Sutton's (2007) work on "The No Asshole Rule" highlights how unchecked negative behaviors can poison entire work environments. Bad bosses create a negative spiral effect throughout the organization, underscoring the critical importance of fostering positive leadership. Sutton's work continued with his book, "Good Boss, Bad Boss," which offers valuable insights into learning from positive and negative leadership experiences. He cites numerous research studies and examples to illustrate key points: Being a jerk is a choice, not an innate trait. Most leaders need help to recognize their actual impact on subordinates. The toxic combination of self-centeredness and obliviousness can devastate organizational culture. He emphasizes that great bosses succeed through consistent, relentless attention to doing one good thing after another, no matter how small. This perspective aligns with the "Best Boss" reflections, highlighting the cumulative impact of positive leadership behaviors.

> Vulnerability in leadership creates a sense of psychological safety that allows others to do the same.

Reflecting on these insights, a powerful principle emerges soft skills create hard results. The qualities participants attribute to their best bosses—empathy, support, and trust—directly correlate with tangible outcomes such as increased engagement, reduced turnover, improved customer satisfaction, and enhanced profitability. This revelation underscores a fundamental truth: as leaders improve, so do their organizations. Better bosses foster better teams, cultures, and better results. This principle will guide us throughout this chapter as we explore the first step in cultivating organizational change: strengthening authentic leadership.

As we delve deeper into this concept, we'll examine strategies for developing these crucial leadership qualities, understanding their impact on organizational dynamics, and learning how to create a positive spiral effect that elevates entire teams and organizations. The journey of authentic leadership begins with self-reflection and a commitment to continuous growth. By embodying the qualities of our "best bosses" and learning from the mistakes of the worst, we can become the leaders our organizations need to thrive in an ever-changing business landscape. Let's embark on this transformative journey together, exploring the power of authentic leadership and its role in shaping organizational culture and success.

The Dimensions of Authentic Leadership: TRIBE

At its core, authentic leadership is about being true to oneself and others. Rooted in the groundbreaking work of Harvard professor Bill George, the founder of Authentic Leadership Theory, this leadership style emphasizes genuineness, ethical behavior, and cultivating positive relationships. While George originally outlined four key components, we're expanding and adapting these elements to create a framework designed to foster workplace positivity. To help leaders easily remember and apply these principles, we've developed the acronym TRIBE. This framework encapsulates the essence of authentic leadership and provides a practical guide for creating a positive, engaged, and high-performing organizational culture. TRIBE stands for:

* Transparency: Open communication and honesty
* Reflection: Self-awareness and continuous personal growth
* Integrity: Ethical decision-making and moral courage
* Balance: Objective analysis and consideration of diverse perspectives
* Empowerment: Enabling others to succeed and reach their potential

Let's explore each of these dimensions in detail and see how they manifest in the day-to-day work of leading an organization.

Transparency: The Foundation of Trust

Transparency in leadership refers to presenting one's authentic self to others. It involves being open and honest in interactions, sharing information freely, and admitting mistakes and limitations. This openness is crucial for building trust and credibility with employees, making leaders feel secure in the trust they've built.

> Authentic leadership is not about perfection, but about understanding your emotions, motivations, strengths, and limitations.

Darin, a COO in the construction industry, emphasizes the importance of transparency in fostering positivity: "I helped influence [positivity] just by respecting the people you're working with, respecting their opinions, respecting their ideas, showing them that you want their ideas, that you want the team efforts, being vulnerable, being open with information."

When leaders are willing to be vulnerable and share their struggles and challenges, it creates a sense of psychological safety that allows others to do the same. This openness helps break down hierarchical barriers, which often contribute to negativity and disengagement.

Heather, another leader, underscores the importance of creating a safe environment: "I think of safety as something that I owe people. Safety is a basic need or a requirement. And if I'm in charge of a team or an environment, I have a leadership responsibility to ensure people are safe.

By being transparent and accessible, authentic leaders convey that everyone's voice and perspective are valued—a foundation for a positive, inclusive workplace culture. This approach fosters open dialogue, encourages feedback, and leads to more robust decision-making and problem-solving within the organization.

Reflection: The Journey of Self-Discovery

Self-awareness, the cornerstone of authentic leadership, is a powerful tool for personal growth and effective leadership. It's not about achieving perfection but understanding one's emotions, motivations, strengths, and limitations. This understanding guides actions and decisions, making it a crucial journey for every leader. Mollie, a leader in her field, aptly points out, "I believe our feelings as leaders are often rooted in unaddressed insecurities. And the reason they're unaddressed often goes back to an unwillingness to be vulnerable with yourself." This insight underscores the importance of introspection and the courage to confront our own vulnerabilities. The benefits of this journey are immense, inspiring leaders to reach new heights in their personal and professional lives.

However, there's often a significant gap between perceived and actual self-awareness among leaders. A Harvard Business Review study revealed a startling reality: only about 15% of people are sufficiently self-aware and less than a 30% correlation exists between people's actual and self-perceived competence. This discrepancy highlights the prevalence of blind spots and the critical need for structured reflection, feedback mechanisms, and openness to change. Tools like 360-degree review assessments can be invaluable in bridging this gap, providing leaders with a comprehensive view of their strengths and areas for improvement from multiple perspectives. As an education leader, Erica emphasizes, "It's about deeply understanding and communicating the purpose behind your actions." This level of clarity comes from consistent self-reflection and a willingness to seek and act on feedback.

The journey of self-discovery is ongoing and requires a commitment to continuous learning and growth. Leaders must be willing to confront their blind spots, challenge their assumptions, and remain open to change. This process of self-awareness is not just beneficial for personal development; it's crucial for effective leadership. As the saying goes, "If you can't lead yourself, how can you lead others?" Self-aware leaders are better equipped to understand and empathize with their team members, make more balanced decisions, and create an environment of trust and authenticity. This emphasis on trust and authenticity in leadership makes team members feel secure and valued, fostering a positive work environment. By embarking on this journey of self-discovery and actively working to close the gap between perceived and actual competence, leaders not only improve their own effectiveness but also inspire and empower those around them to do the same.

Integrity: The Moral Compass

Authentic leadership is anchored in a strong moral perspective—a commitment to doing what is right, even in the face of pressure or adversity. This means having the courage to stand up for one's values, even when they are unpopular or inconvenient.

Stephen, a CEO in the aerospace industry, emphasizes the non-negotiable nature of integrity: "The biggest thing is that you can't compromise on your integrity and integrity values. If you want the company and employees to live to those values, you must be the number one model employee to what those values are."

Authentic leaders understand that their actions speak louder than words and are responsible for modeling the behavior they wish to see in others. This is particularly important when addressing negativity and toxic behavior in the workplace.

Jeff, another CEO, shares his approach to addressing conflict, highlighting the importance of swift action: "I hate conflict. I do. I hate it, but I address it fast because I want it done. I want it done. I want it over."

Authentic leaders communicate that negativity and incivility will not be tolerated by being willing to have difficult conversations and make tough decisions. However, they also understand the importance of approaching these situations with empathy and compassion.

Mollie notes the importance of open-mindedness in these situations: "You must be willing to listen with an open heart and mind. You must listen. You're not going to learn. You won't get to the root of the problem if you can't prove your openness."

By balancing moral courage with emotional intelligence, authentic leaders can navigate complex interpersonal dynamics and create a culture of respect and accountability.

Balance: The Art of Objective Analysis

Another characteristic of authentic leadership is balanced processing—objectively analyzing all relevant data before deciding. This means actively seeking out information that may challenge one's beliefs and being willing to change course based on new insights.

Aaron, a 20-year veteran executive and CEO, shares his perspective on the value of diverse thinking: "If the right leader leans into a pessimistic or a critical thinker, you can learn a lot. You really can. And you can invite that person into your world and rely on them. That's a good thing."

> Balanced processing—objectively analyzing all relevant data before deciding—is a key component of authentic leadership.

Authentic leaders understand that they need all the answers and that the best solutions often emerge from diverse perspectives. They create a culture of intellectual honesty and continuous learning by actively seeking dissenting opinions and encouraging constructive debate.

This approach is essential when it comes to addressing negativity in the workplace. As Peter, an education superintendent, noted: "Negativity is a goldmine of insight about how people are experiencing your leadership and your service."

By being open to feedback, even when it's difficult to hear, authentic leaders can gain valuable insights into the root causes of negativity and develop targeted strategies for addressing it.

Empowerment: Enabling Others to Thrive

The final dimension of authentic leadership focuses on empowering others to succeed and reach their full potential. This involves creating an environment where people feel valued, supported, and encouraged to take initiative and grow. Mel, a Chief People Officer in senior living, emphasizes three key leadership traits:

"Authenticity, vulnerability, and courage are the winning combination. Success follows when you're genuine, open about your limitations, and brave in your actions." By demonstrating these qualities, leaders create an environment where others feel safe to do the same, fostering a culture of trust and openness. They encourage risk-taking, celebrate failures as learning opportunities, and provide the resources and support their team members need to excel. Empowerment also involves recognizing and nurturing each individual's unique strengths and talents. As Erica mentioned, it's about finding your "early adopters" and leveraging their insights and experiences to develop and grow ideas.

Authentic leaders understand that their success is intrinsically linked to their team's success. Empowering others enhances individual performance and fosters a culture of collaboration, innovation, and continuous improvement.

The TRIBE of Authentic Leadership

The TRIBE framework—Transparency, Reflection, Integrity, Balance, and Empowerment—provides a comprehensive guide to authentic leadership. By embodying these principles, leaders can create a positive, productive, and engaging work environment where individuals and the organization can thrive.

Authentic leadership is about more than perfection or having all the answers. Instead, it's about being genuine, ethical, and committed to personal growth and the growth of others. It's about creating a culture of trust, respect, and open communication where diverse perspectives are valued and everyone feels empowered to contribute their best.

As we've seen through the insights shared by various leaders, authentic leadership requires courage, vulnerability, and a willingness to face challenges head-on. It demands a commitment to continuous learning and self-improvement and the ability to balance multiple perspectives and make decisions that align with one's values.

By embracing the TRIBE of authentic leadership, leaders can navigate the complexities of modern organizations, effectively address negativity and toxicity, and create workplaces where people are inspired to do their best work. In doing so, they drive organizational success and contribute to the personal and professional growth of everyone they lead.

Authentic Leadership: A Double-Edged Sword

While authentic leadership has gained significant traction in recent years as a positive force in organizational development, it is essential to examine its potential benefits and drawbacks. This balanced perspective allows us to harness the power of Authenticity while avoiding its potential pitfalls.

The Positive Impact of Authentic Leadership

> Authentic leaders understand that their actions speak louder than words and model the behavior they wish to see in others.

Authentic leadership, characterized by self-awareness, relational transparency, balanced processing, and internalized moral perspective (Walumbwa et al., 2008), has been associated with numerous positive outcomes. Authentic leadership positively influences follower job satisfaction, organizational commitment, and work engagement (Gardner et al. (2011). Furthermore, Avolio and Gardner (2005) argue that authentic leaders foster greater trust, hope, and optimism among their followers, leading to improved organizational performance. Demonstrating that authentic leadership promotes followers' need for satisfaction and work role performance (Leroy et al. (2015). Their study revealed that leaders who exhibit Authenticity create an environment where employees feel more psychologically safe, increasing job satisfaction and productivity.

The Dark Side of Authentic Leadership

As a caution, recent research has also highlighted the potential negative consequences of authentic leadership when misunderstood or misapplied. Alvesson and Einola (2019) critique the concept, arguing that excessive focus on Authenticity can lead to narcissism and self-indulgence among leaders. Nyberg and Sveningsson (2014) caution that pursuing Authenticity can sometimes conflict with effective leadership practices. They argue that leaders may use "being true to oneself" to excuse inflexibility or resistance to necessary change. In a provocative article, Tourish (2019) warns of the "dark side of authentic leadership," suggesting that it can be used to justify authoritarian behaviors. He argues that some leaders may interpret Authenticity as permission to express unfiltered thoughts and emotions, regardless of their impact on others.

Striking a Balance

The key to effectively leveraging authentic leadership lies in understanding its true essence. As George et al. (2007) emphasized, authentic leadership is not about stubbornly adhering to a rigid self-concept but about continuous self-reflection, growth, and adaptation while maintaining core values and ethical standards. Ladkin and Taylor (2010) propose a more nuanced view of authentic leadership, which suggests skillfully aligning one's inner self with external expectations and responsibilities.

This perspective emphasizes that Authenticity in leadership is not about unbridled self-expression but the thoughtful integration of personal values with organizational needs. Ibarra (2015) offers valuable insights into navigating the complexities of authentic leadership. She argues that influential leaders must be willing to adapt and grow, challenging the notion that there is a single "true self" to which one must always adhere. Instead, she proposes that leaders view Authenticity as a dynamic process of aligning their values with the evolving needs of their roles and organizations.

Authentic leadership remains a powerful tool for organizational development when properly understood and applied. However, it is crucial to recognize its limitations and potential misuse. Authentic leadership is not an excuse for poor behavior or inflexibility but a commitment to continuous self-reflection, ethical decision-making, and genuine connection with followers.

As we continue exploring authentic leadership's role in organizational change, we must remember that genuine Authenticity is about character development, not permission for unchecked self-expression. It requires leaders to balance self-awareness with adaptability, transparency with discretion, and personal values with organizational needs. By keeping this balanced perspective, we can harness the transformative power of authentic leadership while avoiding its potential pitfalls, creating more vital, more resilient organizations in the process.

Modeling the Way

Cultivating authentic leadership is not just about developing skills or traits - it's about embodying those qualities in every interaction and decision. Authentic leaders understand that they set the tone for their organizations and that their actions and behaviors profoundly affect the workplace culture. As Darin, the construction COO, said, "Leading by example isn't enough. Many people think, 'If they see me work, they'll learn from it,' but that approach alone doesn't work. You have to be intentional in your leadership." This means being mindful of how one communicates, makes decisions, and shows up in formal and informal interactions. It means consistency in one's values and actions, even when no one is watching.

It also means being willing to own one's mistakes and shortcomings. As Peter, the education superintendent, shared: "Integrity is doing the right thing even when nobody's watching. And I think that's true. But I also think Integrity is doing the right thing when everybody's watching." By modeling vulnerability, Authenticity, and accountability, leaders create a safe space for others to do the same. They foster a culture of trust where people feel comfortable speaking up, taking risks, and learning from failure.

Building Psychological Safety

Authentic leadership aims to create a culture of psychological safety - a shared belief that the team is safe for interpersonal risk-taking. In a psychologically safe environment, people feel comfortable being themselves, expressing their ideas and opinions, and challenging the status quo. As Heather shared: "If everyone in the organization is here, they deserve to be here. I believe that each person is worthy. For everyone to feel safe, they need to feel valued, appreciated, and important enough to be included." Creating this environment requires more than individual Authenticity - a systemic commitment to trust, respect, and inclusion. Leaders must intentionally develop structures and processes that promote open communication, constructive feedback, and collaborative problem-solving.

This might involve regular check-ins and feedback sessions, as Mollie described: "Regularly check in with employees, both individually and as a team, to gauge morale and address concerns." It might involve creating forums for employee voice and participation, as Stephen, the aerospace CEO, suggested: "We need to give every employee at all levels the chance to speak up if something is wrong. It's important to provide everyone with a platform to say, 'I need help' or 'I need to talk to someone.'" It might involve modeling curiosity and openness, as Mel, the senior living Chief People Officer, shared: "When I get inquisitive, it always makes me ask more questions. That curiosity comes through in how I speak and how I act."

By creating a culture of psychological safety, authentic leaders lay the foundation for all other efforts to address negativity and promote positivity in the workplace. They create an environment where people feel valued, respected, and empowered to bring their whole selves to work.

Conclusion

Strengthening authentic leadership is not a one-time event—it's an ongoing process of self-discovery, growth, and learning. It requires a willingness to be vulnerable, embrace discomfort, and lead with courage and compassion. However, as the executives' stories and insights in this chapter demonstrate, the payoff of this work is immense. Leaders can create a ripple effect of positivity and trust throughout their organizations by cultivating self-awareness, relational transparency, balanced processing, and a moral perspective. They can break the cycle of negativity bias and create a culture where everyone feels valued, respected, and empowered to contribute their best work. They can foster the kind of psychological safety that is essential for innovation, collaboration, and growth.

> Fostering authentic leadership is an ongoing process of self-discovery, growth, and learning.

Authentic leadership is just the first step on the journey toward a more positive and resilient workplace culture. In the following chapters, we'll explore the other components of the six-step framework, from reframing mindsets and cultivating psychological capital to addressing negativity constructively and reinforcing positive behaviors. But as we move forward, let us remember the fundamental importance of Authenticity - being true to ourselves and those we lead. Only by bringing our whole, imperfect human selves to the task of leadership can we inspire others to do the same. As Carolyn, a project executive, put it: "I think it just reminds me to give myself the same grace that I give others or try to give others." May we all strive to lead with that same spirit of grace, courage, and Authenticity - and, in so doing, create workplaces where every individual can thrive.

Recap: Step 1 - Strengthening Authentic Leadership

Chapter 3 explores the concept of authentic leadership as a foundational step in fostering positive organizational change. It introduces the TRIBE framework (Transparency, Reflection, Integrity, Balance, and Empowerment) as a guide for leaders to cultivate authenticity and create psychologically safe work environments.

Key Insights:

* Authentic leadership begins with self-reflection and a commitment to continuous personal growth.
* Transparency and vulnerability in leadership are crucial for building trust and

credibility with employees.

* Integrity in leadership involves modeling ethical behavior and addressing conflicts swiftly.
* Balanced processing requires seeking out diverse perspectives and being open to changing course based on new insights.
* Empowering others to succeed is a critical aspect of authentic leadership.
* Authentic leadership can have potential drawbacks if misunderstood or misapplied, such as narcissism or inflexibility.
* Creating psychological safety is essential for strengthening a positive workplace culture where employees feel valued and empowered.

5 Leadership Reflection Questions:

1. How can I better embody the TRIBE framework in my daily leadership practices?
2. In what ways can I create more opportunities for open dialogue and feedback within my team?
3. How might I balance being true to myself with the need for adaptability in my leadership role?
4. What strategies can I implement to foster greater psychological safety within my organization?
5. How can I more effectively use my own vulnerabilities and mistakes as learning opportunities for my team?

Team Exercise: The Authentic Leadership Compass

Objective: To help team members understand and practice the four elements of authentic leadership: self-awareness, relational transparency, balanced processing, and moral perspective.

Materials: Four large posters (one for each element), sticky notes, pens, and a compass (real or drawn).

Time: Approximately 60-90 minutes

Instructions:

1. Set up: Place the four posters in different corners of the room, each labeled with one of the elements of authentic leadership. Draw or place a large compass in the center of the room.

2. Introduction (5 minutes): Explain the four elements of authentic leadership and their importance in creating a positive work environment.

3. Self-Reflection (10 minutes): Ask participants to reflect on their own leadership style and write on sticky notes:

    * A strength related to each element
    * A challenge or area for improvement for each element

4. Compass Navigation (20 minutes):

    * Participants move to the compass in the center.
    * Call out scenarios related to leadership challenges.
    * Participants move to the element they believe is most crucial for addressing that scenario.
    * Discuss why they chose that element and how it applies to the situation.

5. Element Exploration (30 minutes):

    * Divide the team into four groups, each assigned to one element.
    * Groups rotate through each poster, spending 5-7 minutes at each:

        ◦ Discuss the element's importance

        ◦ Share individual experiences related to it

        ◦ Brainstorm strategies to improve this aspect of leadership

        ◦ Groups add their insights to the posters using sticky notes.

6. Gallery Walk (10 minutes):

    * Participants walk around to review all posters and add any concluding thoughts.

7. Reflection and Commitment (15 minutes):

    *Each person shares one key insight they gained and one specific action they commit to taking to enhance their authentic leadership.

8. Closing (5 minutes):

    * Summarize key takeaways and encourage ongoing practice and discussion of authentic leadership.

This exercise engages participants in active learning about all four elements of authentic leadership. It promotes self-reflection, encourages open dialogue, and helps team members understand how these elements apply in real-world scenarios. By the end, participants should have a clearer understanding of authentic leadership and concrete ideas for personal growth.

Chapter 4

Step 2 – Pinpoint Negativity's Impact

IN THE 2024 ANIMATED film *Inside Out 2*, we witness a poignant portrayal of the human psyche when Anxiety, a new emotion, takes control of Riley's mental landscape. This hijacking of Riley's sense of self, beliefs, and moral judgment serves as a perfect metaphor for the psychological death spiral that can afflict not just individuals but entire organizations. Imagine, if you will, that Riley represents a leader within your company. As Anxiety takes hold, we see a vivid illustration of how negative thought patterns can escalate, creating a feedback loop that influences decisions, actions, and the entire organizational Culture. Just as Riley's world is turned upside down by this new, overwhelming emotion, a leader caught in a negativity spiral can inadvertently create a chain reaction that reverberates throughout the company.

The concept of escalation is central to understanding this phenomenon. In *Inside Out 2*, we observe how Anxiety's influence grows exponentially, crowding out other emotions and distorting Riley's perception of reality. Similarly, a leader's initial fear of self-doubt or pessimism in the workplace can quickly snowball. What starts as a minor concern about a project deadline can morph into catastrophic thinking about the company's future. Catastrophic thinking tends to blow things out of proportion, imagining the worst-case scenarios. This can lead to hasty decisions and contagious unease among team members.

This negative feedback loop is particularly insidious in its ability to self-reinforce. As the leader's Anxiety grows, their behavior changes. They might become more controlling, less trusting of their team, or overly critical. These actions, born out of fear and insecurity, often elicit negative responses from employees, further confirming the leader's worst fears and perpetuating the cycle. It is reminiscent of how Riley's attempts to suppress her Anxiety only serve to amplify its power, creating a vicious circle of emotional turmoil. The turmoil can manifest as increased stress, decreased morale, and a general sense of unease in the workplace, further feeding into the leader's Anxiety.

The behavioral consequences of this spiral can be far-reaching within an organization. Just as Riley withdraws from friends and family, a leader caught in this negative loop might isolate themselves from their team, breaking down crucial lines of communication. They might become risk-averse, stifling innovation and growth. Conversely, they might make rash, poorly thought-out decisions to quickly "fix" perceived problems. Sensing this shift, team members may become less engaged, more prone to conflict, or even start looking for new job opportunities, further destabilizing the organization.

Most concerning is the physiological impact of prolonged negativity. Stress, a natural byproduct of Anxiety and negative thinking, takes a toll not just on the individual experiencing it but on everyone in their orbit. In *Inside Out 2*, Riley's emotional well-being is affected by her emotional state. In the workplace, this translates to increased sick days, lowered productivity, and a general atmosphere of burnout. Leaders constantly operating under high stress are likelier to make poor decisions, have difficulty regulating emotions, and maintain healthy work-life boundaries.

> Negativity, left unchecked, can quickly spread and undermine transformation efforts.

This negativity can compound every corner of the organization's Culture if left unchecked. Like a virus, it spreads from person to person, department to department, until the entire company operates under a cloud of pessimism and fear. However, just as Riley learns to integrate Anxiety as a valuable part of her emotional landscape, organizations can also learn to recognize and harness the power of negative emotions. The key lies in awareness—understanding the potential for negativity to spiral out of control and developing strategies to interrupt this cycle before it gains momentum. As leaders, managers, and employees, we all have a role to play in this. Let us take responsibility and empower ourselves to make a positive change. There is hope for a brighter, more optimistic future.

As we have seen, the psychological death spiral can have profound effects on individuals and organizations alike. However, recognizing this impact is only the first step. As we move further into this chapter, we will delve deeper into identifying the signs of a negativity spiral in yourself and others, and we will equip you with practical tools to reframe negative thoughts and emotions, transforming them into catalysts for positive change. Our goal is to shift organizational cultures from ones dominated by fear and doubt to those characterized by resilience, growth, and optimism.

Building on the foundation of authentic leadership we explored in the previous chapter; we now turn our attention to the critical skill of recognizing and addressing negativity in the workplace. While fostering self-awareness, transparency, and moral integrity in leadership is crucial, it is equally essential to develop the ability to identify negativity's presence, understand its root causes, and assess its impact on individuals, teams, and the organization. This is a responsibility we all share.

The second step in our framework is recognizing negativity's impact. Drawing on insights from executive interviews and research in organizational psychology, we will provide a comprehensive picture of negativity in action and the consequences of failing to address it promptly.

> Recognizing negativity's impact requires gathering both quantitative and qualitative data to understand employees' lived experiences.

Moreover, we will review practical strategies for evaluating organizational climate, gathering employee feedback, and diagnosing the root causes of negativity. By the end of this chapter, you will be equipped with a clearer understanding of how to detect negativity in your organization, along with concrete tools to address it effectively. Most importantly, you will gain a renewed conviction about the importance of tackling negativity at its source, preventing it from taking root and spreading throughout your organization.

Neural Soup of Stress

In the aftermath of COVID-19, healthcare professionals navigated uncharted waters; their resilience stretched to the breaking point. Nowhere was this more evident than in the Perioperative department of a bustling hospital, where 60 nurses and support staff grappled with a toxic brew of emotions and challenges that went far beyond mere burnout.

As a consultant brought in to address the urgent and deteriorating situation, I was immediately struck by the palpable tension in the air. The department, once a well-oiled machine, now seemed to be drowning in what I've come to call the "Soup of Stress" – a potent mixture of negativity, heightened anxiety, and fractured relationships that were corroding the very foundation of their work. The staff's collective sentiment was clear: they didn't feel valued, listened to, or supported by their managers, leaders, and physicians. This perceived lack of appreciation had set off a dangerous spiral. Negativity had become the department's lingua franca, with gossip and backbiting replacing professional communication. The stress was not just visible, it was palpable in the tight shoulders, furrowed brows, and weary eyes of the staff.

Neuroscience tells us that chronic stress can literally reshape our brains. As Dr. Curt Thompson notes in "Anatomy of the Soul," prolonged exposure to stress hormones like cortisol can damage the hippocampus, affecting memory and learning. In this Perioperative department, the soup of stress was not just an emotional state – it was potentially altering the neural pathways of the entire staff. The impact of this stress soup was far-reaching. Interdepartmental silos had formed, creating an "us versus them" mentality that hindered collaboration. Bullying incidents were on the rise, further fracturing the team. The connective tissue of empathy and mutual support that once bound the department together was disintegrating. This toxic environment had tangible consequences. Well-being scores plummeted as staff struggled under the weight of their stress. Staffing became a nightmare, with high turnover rates and difficulty attracting new talent. Those who remained were less engaged, their passion for their work dimmed by the constant negativity.

The ripple effects extended to patient care. Surgery scheduling became increasingly chaotic, with delays and cancellations mounting. Patient satisfaction scores took a nosedive as they sensed the underlying tension among the staff caring for them. As I delved deeper, it became clear that the department was caught in a vicious cycle. The more stressed and unhappy the staff became, the more errors and inefficiencies crept into their work. These mistakes then fueled more stress and negativity, creating a self-perpetuating loop of dysfunction.

Breaking this cycle would require more than just surface-level interventions. We needed to address the root causes of the stress soup and fundamentally reshape the department's culture with a comprehensive approach. Drawing on principles of interpersonal neurobiology, we implemented a multifaceted approach. First, we focused on rebuilding trust and communication channels between staff and leadership. We instituted regular listening sessions, giving staff a platform to voice their concerns and feel heard.

Next, we introduced a series of open discussions including giving feedback and gratitude practices to help staff manage stress responses. Simple techniques like reflective exercises and walk-n-talk breaks were integrated into the daily routine, providing moments of calm and perspective in the midst of chaos. We also worked on fostering stronger connections among team members. Team-building exercises were designed for fun and to actively promote empathy and understanding between different roles and departments. Leadership training was crucial. We educated managers and physicians on the neuroscience of stress and the importance of emotional intelligence in creating a positive work environment. They learned techniques for providing meaningful recognition and support to their teams.

Culture change is not an event; it's a process requiring engagement from all stakeholders. Gradually, we began to see shifts in the department's dynamics. The soup of stress started to lose its potency as new, healthier patterns of interaction took hold. Staff reported feeling more valued and supported. Incidents of bullying decreased, and interdepartmental cooperation improved. As the emotional climate shifted, so did the tangible metrics. Well-being scores began to climb. Retention rates stabilized, and the department became more attractive to potential new hires. Engagement levels rose as staff rediscovered their passion for their work. The improvements in the team's functioning directly impacted patient care. Surgery scheduling became more efficient, and patient satisfaction scores began to rebound.

The courage to face the challenges required a collective commitment, the Perioperative department's transformation demonstrated the profound impact of addressing workplace stress at its roots. By understanding and actively working to reshape their "neural soup," they were able to create a healthier, more productive environment—proving that even in the most stressful professions, positive change is possible.

The Signs and Symptoms of Negativity

Negativity in the workplace can manifest in myriad ways, from overt expressions of frustration and conflict to more subtle forms of disengagement and apathy. As a leader, it is critical to be attuned to these signs and symptoms - and rest assured, with the right tools and knowledge, you can notice when something feels "off" in your team or organization. One of the most common manifestations of negativity is a pervasive sense of cynicism or pessimism. Dana, a healthcare industry CEO, said, "You can feel it, and then if you sit in a management meeting, you can tell by the interactions if things are not going well. Are they supportive of each other? Are they laying blame? Are they pointing fingers?"

Blaming, fault-finding, and complaining are often telltale signs that negativity has taken root. When team members constantly focus on what is wrong rather than what is possible, it can quickly sap energy and motivation.

Other signs of negativity might include:

* Increased gossip or rumormongering
* Decreased collaboration or cooperation among team members
* Resistance to change or innovative ideas
* Higher levels of absenteeism or turnover
* A general sense of apathy or disengagement

As Mel put it: "Culture is hard to describe. It is the foundational component, the umbrella over everything, but it is the foundation." When negativity is present, it permeates every aspect of the organizational Culture. Of course, recognizing these signs is only the first step. Leaders must also seek to understand the underlying causes of negativity to address it effectively.

Symptoms and Sources of Workplace Negativity

Negativity in the workplace can stem from a wide range of factors, both individual and organizational. At the individual level, employees may be grappling with personal stressors, such as health issues, financial concerns, or family conflicts. They may feel overwhelmed by the demands of their job or undervalued by their managers and colleagues. At the organizational level, negativity can be fueled by a toxic culture, ineffective leadership, or systemic issues like lack of resources, unclear expectations, or inadequate communication. Common organizational drivers of negativity include:

* Lack of transparency or trust in leadership
* Inconsistent or unfair treatment of employees
* Insufficient recognition or rewards for good work
* Poor work-life balance or excessive workloads
* Unclear or constantly shifting priorities

These factors can create a breeding ground for negativity, as employees feel unsupported, unappreciated, and unable to do their best work. Over time, these feelings can fester and spread, creating a self-perpetuating cycle of disengagement and discontent.

As a nonprofit sector CEO, Steve observed, "I believe there is increased stress and anxiety. People generally have a different attitude toward work, work-life balance, and companies." In other words, the roots of negativity are often complex and multifaceted, reflecting broader societal shifts and organizational dynamics.

The Costs of Ignoring Negativity

As I sat across from Chris, the VP of Operations at a prominent university hospital, I could sense the weight of concern in his voice. "The negativity in our operating rooms is costing us more than morale," he said. "It impacts patient care, staff retention, and our bottom line. We need to see a change for the better, but where do we start?" Chris's predicament is far from unique in the healthcare industry, especially after the COVID-19 pandemic. The operating room, a high-stakes environment where precision and teamwork are paramount, has become a breeding ground for negativity. Tensions between physicians, nurses, managers, and directors have escalated, creating a toxic atmosphere that reverberates throughout the hospital system.

Recent research has shed light on the pervasive nature of negativity bias in workplace settings, particularly in high-stress environments like healthcare. A study by Kaplan et al. (2018) demonstrated that negative information is weighed more heavily than positive information in performance evaluations, leading to skewed perceptions and decreased morale. When left unchecked, this bias erodes trust, hampers communication, and compromises patient care.

> Examining how organizational systems, processes, and norms may inadvertently reinforce negativity is essential.

The cost of this negativity is staggering. A 2022 workplace study revealed that 52% of employees leave their jobs due to negative cultural norms and feeling undervalued by their organization or management (Kuzior et al., 2022). In the healthcare sector, where staffing shortages were already a critical issue pre-pandemic, this turnover can have dire consequences. The loss of experienced healthcare professionals impacts patient care quality and places an enormous financial burden on hospitals regarding recruitment and training costs. Moreover, the shift to hybrid work models and increased stress levels due to the pandemic have exacerbated interpersonal conflicts and communication breakdowns (Landolfi et al., 2021). In an operating room setting, where clear communication and seamless teamwork are essential, these issues can lead to medical errors, compromised patient safety, and increased hospital liability risks.

The financial implications of negativity extend beyond turnover and liability. Research has shown that negative workplace cultures decrease productivity, increase absenteeism, and lower patient satisfaction scores (Wax et al., 2022). These factors can translate into millions of dollars in lost revenue and reimbursements for a university hospital like Chris's. However, amidst these challenges lies an opportunity for transformative change. My dissertation research and recent studies on positive organizational behavior suggest that executive leaders are crucial in shifting workplace cultures from negative to positive. By implementing strategies that foster psychological safety, promote open communication, and cultivate employee well-being, healthcare leaders can create resilient, engaged teams better equipped to handle the complex challenges of modern healthcare delivery.

As I began to outline potential strategies for Chris and his team, it became clear that addressing negativity in the operating room was not just about improving workplace dynamics—it was about safeguarding patient lives, preserving the mental health of healthcare professionals, and ensuring the long-term sustainability of the hospital. The journey ahead would be challenging, but the cost of inaction was too high to ignore. However, given the complexity of these underlying factors, it can be tempting for leaders to ignore or minimize the signs of negativity in their organizations. Dealing with these issues can be uncomfortable, time-consuming, and emotionally draining. However, as the executives I interviewed emphasized, the costs of ignoring negativity are alarmingly high. When leaders fail to pinpoint and address negativity, it can rapidly spiral out of control, infecting every aspect of the organization. As Darin, a COO, put it: "If you don't address it, negativity becomes the default culture, influencing how employees think, feel, and behave."

The consequences of this kind of toxic Culture are far-reaching. At the individual level, negativity can lead to increased stress, burnout, and employee disengagement. As Aaron, a healthcare CEO, shared: "If you lack the internal resources, you won't be able to achieve your goals. If you're not paying attention, that stress can build up to a tipping point, leaving you with neither the time nor the energy to perform at your best. "When employees constantly battle negativity, they do not have the energy or motivation to bring their best selves to work. At the team level, negativity can erode trust, collaboration, and innovation. When team members are focused on placing blame or protecting their interests, they are less likely to work together effectively or take risks on innovative ideas. As Erica mentioned, "When trust and collaboration are lacking, I remember instances when a teacher would discuss another teacher negatively. My first question would always be, 'Have you talked to that teacher?' One of our core values is to maintain professional dialogue with one another, even when it's uncomfortable."

As an education superintendent, Peter observed, "Every system is perfectly designed for the results that it produces." When negativity festers, it can lead to increased turnover, decreased productivity, and failure to achieve critical goals. In short, ignoring negativity is not an option for leaders who want to build thriving, resilient organizations. As CEO Jeff said: "You can see, smell, feel, and hear it." When it is there, you know it is there. There is something that's not right."

Assessing the Organizational Climate

> Leaders must acknowledge their own role in perpetuating negativity and be open to feedback on how their actions contribute to the climate.

So how can leaders effectively assess the level of negativity in their organizations - and identify the root causes behind it? The executives I interviewed offered a range of strategies and approaches. One of the most common themes was the importance of regularly engaging with employees at all levels of the organization. Heather, from the construction industry, shared her approach: "I observed meetings carefully. I arranged joint meetings with two team members so they could give each other feedback. When I shared very different feedback, they didn't believe me. So, I asked several project team members how things were going."

Leaders can gain a more accurate view of the organizational climate by actively seeking employee feedback

Through one-on-one conversations, team meetings, or anonymous surveys—leaders can get a more accurate picture of the organizational climate and identify potential areas of concern. Other strategies for assessing negativity might include:

* Monitoring key metrics like employee turnover, absenteeism, or customer complaints
* Conducting regular engagement surveys or pulse checks
* Encouraging open communication and feedback through multiple channels
* Paying attention to nonverbal cues and body language in meetings and interactions
* Seeking input from external stakeholders or partners

The key is to approach this assessment with curiosity and openness. Avoid defensiveness or blame. Heather expressed this idea: "I focus on being curious and receptive, not on avoiding defensiveness. Sometimes, it means making tough decisions. People may dislike these choices now, but they make a difference in the long term."

Conclusion

Just like Riley from *Inside Out 2* demonstrates, recognizing the impact of negativity in the workplace is not always easy—it requires a willingness to confront unchecked emotions and uncomfortable truths, have difficult conversations, and make tough decisions. However, as the executives' stories and insights in this chapter demonstrate, building a positive, resilient organizational culture is essential. By proactively assessing the organizational climate, seeking out employee feedback, and identifying the root causes of negativity, leaders can nip potential problems before they spiral out of control. They can create a culture where negativity cannot fester and positivity, trust, and collaboration can flourish.

Of course, recognizing negativity is just the first step—leaders must also be equipped with the strategies and tools to address it effectively. In the following chapters, we will explore some of these strategies in more depth, from reframing negative mindsets to promoting psychological safety and resilience. However, the message is clear for now: ignoring negativity is not an option. As leaders, we are responsible for creating workplaces where every individual can thrive - and that starts with being willing to confront negativity head-on, with courage, compassion, and a commitment to positive change.

Recap: Step 2 - Pinpoint Negativity's Impact

This chapter explored the critical importance of recognizing and addressing negativity in the workplace, using the metaphor of *Inside Out* 2 to illustrate how negative thought patterns can escalate and impact an entire organization.

Key Insights:

* Negativity can create a self-reinforcing cycle that impacts individual and organizational performance.
* Leaders play a crucial role in recognizing and addressing negativity before it spreads.
* Signs of negativity include increased gossip, decreased collaboration, resistance to change, and higher turnover.
* The roots of negativity can be individual (personal stressors) and organizational (toxic culture, ineffective leadership).
* Ignoring negativity can lead to decreased productivity, increased turnover, and compromised quality of work.
* Assessing organizational climate through employee feedback, metrics, and observation is crucial for identifying negativity.
* Addressing negativity requires a proactive, curious, and open approach from leaders.

STEP 2 - PINPOINT NEGATIVITY'S IMPACT

5 Leadership Reflection Questions:

1. How attuned am I to the signs of negativity in my team or organization? What indicators might I be overlooking?
2. How might my behavior or leadership style contribute to or mitigate negativity in the workplace?
3. How effectively am I gathering and responding to employee feedback about the organizational climate?
4. What strategies have I implemented to pinpoint the impact of negativity, and how successful have they been?
5. How can I create a more open and psychologically safe environment where team members feel comfortable discussing concerns?

Team Discussion Exercise: Negativity Mapping

Objective: To collectively identify and address sources of negativity in the workplace.

Materials: Large whiteboard or flipchart, markers, sticky notes

Instructions:

1. Divide the team into small groups of 3-4 people.
2. Ask each group to brainstorm and list on sticky notes:

a) Signs of negativity they've observed in the workplace

b) Potential root causes of these negative elements

c) Impacts of this negativity on individuals, teams, and the organization

3. Have groups place sticky notes on the whiteboard, clustering similar ideas.
4. As an entire team, review the clusters and discuss:

- Which areas of negativity seem most prevalent or impactful?
- Are there any surprising patterns or insights?
- How might these negative elements be interconnected?

5. Now, have the groups brainstorm potential solutions or strategies to address the top 3-5 areas of negativity identified.
6. Share these strategies with the whole team and discuss their feasibility and potential impact.
7. Conclude by having each team member commit to one action they will take to help address negativity in the workplace.

This exercise helps teams collectively pinpoint the signs and impacts of negativity while empowering them to be part of the solution. It promotes open dialogue about challenging topics and encourages a proactive approach to creating a more positive workplace culture.

Chapter 5
Step 3 - Influence Positive Mindsets

THE SOFT HUM OF the engine filled our Navigator as we cruised down the familiar streets of our neighborhood. In the back seat, strapped securely in his car seat, sat our three-year-old son, Grady. Unlike his sisters, who often succumbed to the lull of car rides and drifted into deep naps, Grady was wide-eyed and alert, his gaze fixed on the world outside his window. From an early age, Grady displayed an uncanny awareness of his surroundings. Even before he could form complete sentences, he could provide directions from the backseat if he knew our destination. He had an internal GPS, always attuned to our route and purpose.

However, one thing invariably disrupted Grady's calm demeanor during these car rides: the dreaded U-turn. Whenever circumstances required us to change direction, an alarm would go off in Grady's brain. His distress was evident, and we'd hear about it until we reached our destination. Something had changed without his permission or understanding, which deeply unsettled him.

Grady's reaction to these unexpected changes in direction offers a poignant metaphor for how we often respond to shifts in our professional lives. How do you feel when you're headed one way and suddenly something changes? In the workplace, we agree to a job, project, or goal, working with a team, and then suddenly, what we said yes turns out to be quite different than expected. Like Grady, no one consulted us about the change, and explanations often come after we've reacted emotionally. However, these unexpected changes also present opportunities for growth and learning, if we can reframe our mindset to see them as such.

Mindsets and expectations are powerful predictors of the outcomes of our work and the dynamics within our teams. They shape our perceptions, influence our behaviors, and determine our ability to adapt and thrive in the face of change. Yet, as Grady's story illustrates, these mindsets can be deeply ingrained and resistant to change.

> Reframing is not a one-time event—it's an ongoing process that requires consistent effort and attention.

We explored the importance of recognizing negativity's impact on the workplace. Leaders can better understand the challenges facing their organizations by being attuned to the signs and symptoms of negativity, seeking out employee feedback, and identifying the root causes of discontent. As we've seen throughout this book, leaders have a crucial role in transforming a negative culture into a positive one. It's not enough to be aware of negativity; leaders must be proactive in inspiring a move toward positivity, leaving negativity behind. The requires reframing mindsets, shifting narratives, and setting clear expectations for communication and behavior.

The third step in our framework, inspiring positive mindsets, focuses on this. In this chapter, we'll explore the power of mental models and cognitive frames to shape our work experiences and leaders' role in influencing these models for better or worse. Our strategies for inspiring positive mindsets are not just theoretical concepts; they are practical tools drawn from cognitive psychology, neuroscience, and organizational behavior, as well as the real-world experiences of the executives I interviewed. These strategies are designed to shift negative narratives, promote a growth mindset, and foster resilience in facing challenges and setbacks.

By the end of this chapter, you'll understand how to harness the power of inspiration through the use of reframing and its potential to create a more positive, adaptable, and mentally healthy workplace culture. These changes have significant benefits and can lead to improved employee well-being and productivity.

The Power of Mental Models

Mental models are at the heart of the reframing process - the cognitive frameworks and assumptions that shape how we perceive, interpret, and respond to the world around us. As the renowned psychologist and Nobel laureate Daniel Kahneman explains in his book "Thinking, Fast and Slow," our minds constantly create coherent stories and explanations based on the limited information available. These mental models serve as shortcuts, allowing us to understand complex situations quickly and efficiently. But they can also lead us astray, based on faulty assumptions, incomplete data, or negative biases.

Negative mental models can be particularly damaging in the workplace. When employees view their jobs, colleagues, or organizations through cynicism, mistrust, or helplessness, it colors every interaction and decision. Small setbacks feel like catastrophes; minor slights feel like personal attacks, and the possibility of positive change feels remote. As Mel put it, "It's all about the spiral. It's all about the spiraling up of the dialogue versus the spiraling down. People love to spiral down because it feels better. And it's harder to spiral up."

Negativity can become a self-fulfilling prophecy - a default way of thinking and behaving that reinforces itself over time. Breaking this cycle requires a concerted effort to reframe mindsets and expectations - deliberately shifting the narrative from negative to positive.

Polarity of Mindset

Early this Spring, Cari and I welcomed a group of 25 young adults into our home. The living room buzzed with energy as recent graduates and young professionals settled in, balancing plates of snacks and cups of iced tea. The air was filled with excitement and uncertainty - perfectly reflecting their current life stage.

As everyone found their seats, I couldn't help but notice the subtle dynamics at play. Some clustered in familiar groups, while others tentatively introduced themselves to unfamiliar faces. The room was a microcosm of the challenges these twenty-somethings faced daily: the pursuit of independence, the weight of financial responsibilities, the complexities of friendships and romantic relationships, and the ongoing journey of self-discovery.

I began the evening by introducing our topic: mindset, as viewed through the lens of Romans 8. The biblical text, written two millennia ago, held surprising relevance to the mental health challenges of today. To kick off our discussion, I asked, "What does mindset mean to you?"

The room came alive with responses. Some spoke of attitude, others of perspective. A few mentioned habits and thought patterns. It was clear that everyone had their understanding shaped by individual experiences and challenges.

To delve deeper, I introduced a series of comparisons, asking the group to imagine each pair as opposite ends of a spectrum:

1. Half-empty or half-full
2. Scarcity vs. abundance
3. Yes vs. No
4. Optimistic vs. pessimistic
5. Surviving vs. thriving
6. Life-minded vs. death-minded
7. Growth vs. fixed

As we explored each comparison, the discussion grew more animated. A recent graduate spoke about her struggle with a scarcity mindset as she navigated the job market. A young software engineer shared how adopting a growth mindset had transformed his career. A newly dating couple discussed how their differing perspectives - one more optimistic, the other more pessimistic - affected their relationship. Cari, ever observant, gently steered the conversation when it veered off course, ensuring everyone had a chance to contribute. Her warm presence encouraged even the quietest participants to share their thoughts.

As the evening progressed, we delved into the biblical perspective on mindset, drawing parallels between Paul's teachings in Romans 8 and modern psychological concepts. The group was particularly struck by the idea of a "life-minded" versus "death-minded" outlook, relating it to their own experiences with anxiety and depression.

One young woman, a mental health advocate, shared how shifting from a surviving mindset to a thriving mindset had been crucial in her recovery from burnout. Her story resonated deeply with many in the room, sparking a heartfelt discussion about the pressures of early adulthood and the importance of mental well-being.

> Shift from a scarcity mindset focused on problems to an abundance mindset concentrating on possibilities and strengths.

As the night ended, the energy in the room had shifted. What began as a gathering of individuals grappling with their challenges had transformed into a community of support and understanding. The ancient words of Romans 8 sparked a thoroughly modern conversation about mindset, resilience, and hope.

Cari and I exchanged glances as we watched the last of our guests depart, still deep in conversation. We knew that while we couldn't solve all the challenges these young adults faced, we had provided a space for reflection, connection, and growth. And we had helped them navigate the complex journey of finding their place in the world, armed with a new perspective on the power of mindset.

The Complexity of Mindset at Work

Building on our exploration of mindsets, let's delve into how these mental frameworks manifest in the workplace and their profound implications for leadership, teamwork, and organizational culture. We'll examine seven key mindset categories: Half-Empty vs. Half-Full, Scarcity vs. Abundance, Yes vs. No, Optimistic vs. Pessimistic, Surviving vs. Thriving, Life-Minded vs. Death-Minded, and Growth vs. Fixed.

The Half-Empty vs. Half-Full mindset reflects a tendency to focus on negatives or shortcomings versus an inclination to see positives and opportunities. In the workplace, those with a half-empty mindset often exhibit frequent complaints and resistance to change, while those with a half-full perspective are solution-oriented and adaptable. A study by Lyubomirsky et al. (2005) in the Review of General Psychology found that positive emotions and optimism are linked to success across multiple life domains, including work performance. Leaders with a "half-full" mindset tend to inspire and motivate teams, fostering a culture of resilience and innovation.

The Scarcity vs. Abundance mindset revolves around the belief that resources (time, opportunities, recognition) are limited versus the perception that there are ample resources and opportunities for all. Those with a scarcity mindset often hoard information and are reluctant to delegate, while those with an abundance mindset tend to be collaborative and empowering. Mullainathan and Shafir's book "Scarcity: Why Having Too Little Means So Much" (2013) discusses how a scarcity mindset can lead to poor decision-making and reduced cognitive capacity. An abundance mindset fosters a collaborative culture where knowledge sharing is the norm, encouraging innovation and cross-functional teamwork.

The Yes vs. No mindset distinguishes between those who are open to new ideas and possibilities and those who are resistant to change. In the workplace, a "yes" mindset manifests enthusiasm about new projects and proactive problem-solving, while a "no" mindset tends to be risk-averse and quick to dismiss innovative ideas. Grant and Gino's 2010 study in the Journal of Personality and Social Psychology found that a culture of gratitude and positivity (aligned with a "Yes" mindset) increased prosocial behavior in the workplace. A "Yes" mindset in leadership can create a culture of innovation and calculated risk-taking.

The Optimistic vs. Pessimistic mindset contrasts the expectation of positive outcomes with the anticipation of negative ones. Optimistic individuals tend to be resilient in the face of setbacks, while pessimistic ones are easily discouraged. Seligman's work on learned optimism, detailed in his book "Learned Optimism" (1991), shows how optimism can be cultivated and its positive effects on performance and well-being. Optimistic leaders build more resilient teams that can bounce back from setbacks, leading to increased productivity and better stress management.

The Surviving vs. Thriving mindset differentiates between focusing on meeting basic needs and maintaining the status quo versus emphasizing growth and exceeding expectations. Those in survival mode often exert minimal effort and resist additional responsibilities, while those thriving are proactive and seek learning opportunities. Spreitzer and Porath's research, summarized in their Harvard Business Review article "Creating Sustainable Performance" (2012), shows that employees who are "thriving" demonstrate 16% better overall performance. A thriving mindset at all levels of an organization can led to higher engagement and a culture of continuous improvement.

The Life-Minded vs. Death-Minded perspective contrasts a focus on growth and possibilities with a preoccupation with limitations and adverse outcomes. Life-minded individuals tend to be forward-thinking and purpose-driven, while death-minded ones are often risk-averse and lack enthusiasm. In his book "Life Minded," Pastor Brady Boyd explores how a life-minded perspective can transform one's outlook and actions, leading to more fulfilling and purposeful living. This concept extends to the workplace, where a life-minded approach can invigorate teams and drive meaningful work.

Finally, the Growth vs. Fixed mindset, as popularized by Carol Dweck in her book "Mindset: The New Psychology of Success" (2006), contrasts the belief that abilities can be developed through effort and learning with the belief that they are static and unchangeable. Those with a growth mindset embrace challenges and seek feedback, while those with a fixed mindset often avoid challenges and are defensive to feedback. Organizations that foster a growth mindset tend to see higher employee engagement and innovation levels.

The mindsets we cultivate in the workplace have far-reaching effects on individual performance, team dynamics, and overall organizational culture. Leaders can create more positive, productive, and purposeful work environments by understanding and actively shaping these mindsets. The challenge lies in recognizing our mindsets and consciously working to adopt more beneficial perspectives, not just for personal growth but for the collective success of our teams and organizations.

Shifting the Narrative

So, how can leaders shift negative narratives in their organizations? The executives I interviewed offered a range of strategies and approaches, but one common theme emerged: the power of language and communication. Mel explained, "It's all about the language, number one, and number two is behavior." How we talk about our work, colleagues, and challenges profoundly impacts how we think and feel about them. This realization empowers leaders to influence the narrative in their organizations, fostering a more positive and productive work environment.

One simple but powerful technique for shifting language is to reframe problems as opportunities. Instead of focusing on what's wrong or not working, leaders can encourage their teams to look for the potential benefits or lessons in every challenge. For example, when faced with a complex customer complaint, a leader might say, "This is a chance for us to understand our customers' needs and find new ways to exceed their expectations," instead of, "Great, another angry customer to deal with." This subtle shift in framing can significantly impact employees' approach to work. As an education superintendent, Peter said, "Negativity is a goldmine of insight about how people are experiencing your leadership and your service." By reframing negative feedback as valuable data, leaders can help their teams focus on continuous improvement and growth. This role in fostering a positive work environment is crucial and valued. Another way to shift narratives is to celebrate successes and progress, no matter how small. In a hostile culture, it's easy to fixate on failures and shortcomings while ignoring or downplaying achievements. However, leaders can create a counter-narrative of positivity and momentum by actively looking for and acknowledging the good.

Heather, shared how her organization does this through regular gratitude practices: "We hold leadership huddles with individuals from across the organization, starting with participants sharing what they are grateful for or how they would like to celebrate someone else." By institutionalizing gratitude and celebration, leaders send a powerful message about what matters - and help shift the focus from deficits to strengths.

Setting Clear Expectations

Reframing mindsets is not just about shifting language—it's also about setting clear, constructive expectations for behavior and communication. Negativity often takes hold in an organization because there are no explicit norms or guidelines for how people should interact and work together. As Erica, an education leader, explained, "I think about core values as giving them permission to be innovative and talk collaboratively so that we can use the collective genius of our work to best serve those that we're serving." By establishing shared values and principles - and consistently modeling and reinforcing them - leaders take responsibility for creating a framework for positive, productive behavior, thereby influencing the organizational culture. Some key expectations that can help counter negativity include:

> Set clear, constructive expectations for behavior and communication to counter negativity.

* Treat all colleagues respectfully and professionally, even when disagreements or conflicts occur.
* Communicating openly and honestly, focusing on solutions rather than blame.
* Being willing to have difficult conversations and provide constructive feedback, but always with the intent of helping others grow and improve.
* Taking ownership and accountability for one's work and behavior rather than making excuses or pointing fingers.
* Seeking out diverse perspectives and valuing the contributions of all team members.

This practice not only fosters a more inclusive and open-minded culture but also encourages innovation and creativity, making leaders feel more connected to their teams and the broader organizational mission.

Promoting a Growth Mindset

A crucial aspect of reframing mindsets is promoting a growth mindset - believing skills and abilities can be developed through hard work, learning, and persistence. As Stanford psychologist Carol Dweck explains in her book "Mindset," individuals with a growth mindset see challenges and failures as opportunities to learn and improve rather than threats to their self-worth or competence. A growth mindset fosters resilience, adaptability, and innovation in the workplace. When employees believe they can grow and develop, they are more likely to take risks, embrace feedback, and bounce back from setbacks.

> Promote a growth mindset—the belief that abilities can be developed through effort, learning, and persistence.

Unfortunately, many organizational cultures inadvertently promote a fixed mindset - the belief that abilities are innate and unchangeable.

This can happen through performance review systems that focus solely on past achievements or through a lack of opportunities for learning and development. To counter this, leaders can actively promote a growth mindset by:

* Emphasizing the value of learning, experimentation, and continuous improvement.
* Providing regular opportunities for skill development and career growth.
* Giving constructive, forward-looking feedback focusing on effort and progress, not just outcomes.
* Celebrating "intelligent failures" and the lessons learned from them.
* Modeling a growth mindset in their behavior and communication.

As a nonprofit CEO, Steve expressed, "Having faith in God is essential. I can't imagine leading without that faith, as fear and negativity can easily take over." While not all leaders may share Steve's religious beliefs, the underlying principle is the same: a deep belief in the power of growth, learning, and persistence, is essential even in the face of adversity.

Fostering Resilience

Resiliency is closely related to the growth mindset concept—the capacity to bounce back from challenges, setbacks, and failures. In an increasingly volatile, uncertain, complex, and ambiguous workplace (VUCA), resilience has become an essential leadership competency and organizational imperative. As Eric, a construction industry executive, shared, "I can control destiny because I have the resources I need now." In other words, resilience is not just about having a positive attitude—it's about having the tangible and intangible resources needed to navigate demanding situations and emerge stronger on the other side. So, how can leaders foster resilience in themselves and their teams? Some key strategies include:

> Foster resilience by building strong support networks, developing a sense of purpose, and practicing self-care.

* Building solid and supportive relationships and networks.
* Developing a sense of purpose and meaning in one's work.
* Cultivating self-awareness and emotional intelligence.
* Practicing self-care and stress management techniques.
* Encouraging a culture of openness, transparency, and psychological safety.
* Providing the necessary resources, tools, and support for success.

By creating an environment supporting resilience and modeling resilient behaviors, leaders can help their teams navigate the most demanding challenges with confidence and grace.

Conclusion

Reframing mindsets and expectations are critical to a more positive, resilient workplace culture. By shifting negative narratives, setting clear expectations, promoting a growth mindset, and fostering resilience, leaders can create an environment where employees feel empowered, supported, and motivated to bring their best selves to work. But as we've seen throughout this chapter, reframing is not a one-time event—it's a process. Leaders must be vigilant in monitoring their language and behavior and that of their teams. They must also proactively identify and challenge negative mental models and create opportunities for learning, growth, and resilience.

The power of reframing lies in its ability to tap into the fundamental human capacity for change and adaptation. As leaders, we have the opportunity - and the responsibility - to harness this capacity to provide a better, more positive, and more fulfilling workplace experience. So, let us commit to the challenging work of reframing—to shifting our mindsets and expectations first and then helping others do the same. Let us believe in the power of growth, resilience, and positive transformation. And let us never underestimate how a single word, interaction, or shift in perspective can impact those we lead.

Recap: Step 3 - Inspire Positive Mindsets

This chapter focused on inspiring mindsets and expectations to transform negative workplace cultures into positive ones.

STEP 3 - INFLUENCE POSITIVE MINDSETS

Key Insights:

* Mental models shape how we perceive and respond to our work environment.
* Shifting language and communication can powerfully reframe negative narratives.
* Setting clear, positive expectations for behavior and communication is crucial.
* Promoting a growth mindset fosters resilience, adaptability, and innovation.
* Resilience is an essential leadership competency in today's VUCA world.
* Inspiring is an ongoing process that requires consistent effort and attention.
* Leaders play a vital role in modeling and reinforcing positive mindsets.

5 Leadership Reflection Questions:

1. How often do I consciously reframe negative situations into opportunities for growth or learning?

2. In what ways do I promote a growth mindset within my team? Are there areas where I might be inadvertently reinforcing a fixed mindset?

3. How clear and consistent are the expectations I set for positive behavior and communication in my team?

4. How do I personally model resilience in the face of challenges, and how can I better support my team in developing resilience?

5. What strategies can I implement to celebrate successes and progress, no matter how small, more regularly?

Team Discussion Exercise: Inspiring Challenges

Objective: To practice reframing negative situations into opportunities for growth and learning.

Materials: Whiteboard or flip chart, markers, sticky notes

Instructions:

1. Divide the team into small groups of 3-4 people.

2. Ask each group to write down 3-5 recent challenges or setbacks the team or organization has faced on sticky notes (one per note).

3. Have groups place their sticky notes on a shared board.

4. As a full team, choose 5-6 diverse challenges from the board.

5. For each selected challenge, have the groups work together to
   a) Identify the negative narrative or mindset associated with this challenge
   b) Reframe the situation positively, focusing on opportunities for growth, learning, or improvement
   c) Suggest specific actions that could be taken based on this reframed perspective.

6. Have each group present their reframes and action steps to the full team.

7. Discuss as a full group:
   • Which reframes were most impactful or surprising?
   • How might adopting these reframed perspectives change how the team approaches challenges?
   • What strategies can the team use to inspire more positvity in their day-to-day work?

8. Conclude by having each team member share one insight they

gained from the exercise and one reframing technique they commit to practicing in the coming week.

This exercise helps teams practice the skill of reframing, encourages collaborative problem-solving, and promotes a more positive, growth-oriented approach to workplace challenges.

Chapter 6
Step 4 - Rebuild Psychological Capital

IN TODAY'S RAPIDLY CHANGING and often challenging work environments, cultivating psychological capital (PsyCap) has become essential for individual and organizational success. As leaders, we are responsible for fostering PsyCap, a concept rooted in positive psychology that focuses on developing an individual's positive psychological state characterized by hope, efficacy, resilience, and optimism (Luthans et al., 2007). This chapter explores how we can do this for ourselves and our teams, creating more engaged, productive, and resilient workplaces.

The importance of PsyCap in the modern workplace cannot be overstated. Recent studies have revealed that PsyCap is positively associated with work engagement and negatively associated with burnout (Saeed et al., 2023). Maintaining a positive outlook and bouncing back from setbacks is crucial in an era marked by rapid technological change, economic uncertainty, and global challenges like the COVID-19 pandemic.

Consider the story of Sarah, a newly promoted executive at a rapidly growing tech company. Sarah faced a perfect storm of challenges as she entered her new role. Externally, the market was becoming increasingly competitive, with new disruptive technologies threatening their market share. Internally, the company needed help with growing pains, including communication breakdowns between departments and resistance to necessary organizational changes. These challenges were not unique to Sarah's situation but indicated the complex, high-pressure environments many leaders find themselves in. Sarah's initial days were marked by uncertainty, stress, and a constant struggle to prove herself in the face of these challenges.

> Psychological capital - hope, efficacy, resilience, and optimism - is a powerful resource for leaders navigating complex negative environments.

When Sarah first stepped into her new role, she felt the weight of her responsibilities. The stress of navigating these complex challenges while proving herself in her new role was taking a toll. She found herself second-guessing her decisions, struggling to inspire her team, and feeling overwhelmed by the constant pressure to perform.

Recognizing the need for support, Sarah engaged me as her executive coach. In this role, I provided guidance and support as we worked together to rebuild her psychological capital (PsyCap) to help her cope with these challenges and thrive in her new role. We began by working on Sarah's hope. Together, we set clear, achievable goals for her personal leadership development and organizational objectives. She set clear goals and instilled a sense of focus and determination, which are vital in her journey to rebuild PsyCap and thrive in her new role.

To build her self-efficacy, we reviewed her past successes and identified the skills that had led to her promotion. We then created a plan to develop further the competencies she needed in her new role, such as strategic thinking and change management. As Sarah successfully tackled increasingly challenging tasks, her confidence in leading at this higher level grew. Resilience became a key focus as Sarah faced setbacks and obstacles. We reframed these challenges as opportunities for growth and learning. Sarah began to view difficulties not as personal failures but as natural parts of the leadership journey. She developed strategies to bounce back quickly from setbacks and maintain her motivation in the face of adversity.

Finally, we worked on cultivating Sarah's optimism. This was not about ignoring problems or maintaining unrealistic positivity. Instead, Sarah learned to realistically assess situations while focusing on opportunities and solutions rather than dwelling on problems.

As Sarah's PsyCap grew, the impact on her leadership was profound. She approached challenges with a more balanced and confident perspective. Her team began to respond to her newfound assurance, becoming more engaged and innovative. Sarah's improved communication skills, bolstered by her increased confidence, helped her bridge gaps between departments and rallied the organization around necessary changes. For instance, she implemented a new communication strategy that significantly improved interdepartmental collaboration.

Even as market pressures intensified, Sarah was able to lead with clarity and purpose. She inspired her team to embrace innovation and adapt to changing market conditions. Her resilience in the face of setbacks became a model for the entire organization. Through our coaching relationship and her dedication to personal growth, Sarah transformed from a stressed, uncertain new executive to a confident, inspiring leader. Her journey vividly illustrates the transformative power of cultivating PsyCap on leadership effectiveness, especially when facing complex, multifaceted challenges in a high-pressure environment. This should inspire and instill a sense of hope and optimism in leaders, showing them the potential for their own PsyCap journey and igniting a fire of inspiration and motivation.

PsyCap by the Numbers

Sarah's journey demonstrates the transformative power of cultivating psychological capital in leadership. Her experience is not unique; numerous studies have shown the significant impact of PsyCap on individual leaders and organizational outcomes. Let us explore five critical outcomes supported by empirical research:

1. Increased Employee Engagement: A meta-analysis by Saeed et al. (2023) found a strong positive correlation between PsyCap and work engagement. Organizations with leaders high in PsyCap reported up to 30% higher employee engagement scores than those with low PsyCap leaders. This increased engagement translates to improved productivity and job satisfaction.

2. Enhanced Leadership Effectiveness: Research by Niswaty et al. (2021) revealed that authentic leadership, closely tied to high PsyCap, directly predicts work engagement. Leaders with high PsyCap scores were rated 25% more effective by their teams than those with low PsyCap scores.

3. Reduced Burnout and Turnover: The 2023 meta-study also showed that PsyCap was negatively associated with burnout. Organizations that implemented PsyCap development programs reported a 20% decrease in burnout symptoms among employees and a 15% reduction in turnover rates over one year.

4. Improved Team Performance: A study by Ciftci and Erkanli (2020) found that teams led by high-PsyCap leaders demonstrated 18% higher performance ratings and were 22% more likely to meet or exceed their goals than teams led by low-PsyCap leaders.

5. Increased Innovation and Adaptability: Research by Shahid and Muchiri (2019) showed that organizations with elevated levels of PsyCap among their leadership were 35% more likely to implement innovative strategies successfully and 27% more adaptable to market changes than their low-PsyCap counterparts.

> Organizations with elevated levels of PsyCap are 35% more likely to implement innovative strategies successfully.

These statistics underscore the critical role of PsyCap in today's dynamic business environment. By investing in the development of psychological capital, organizations can create a more resilient, engaged, and high-performing workforce capable of navigating the challenges of the modern business landscape.

In the following sections, we will delve deeper into each component of PsyCap - hope, efficacy, resilience, and optimism - and provide practical strategies for cultivating these qualities in yourself and your team. By understanding and applying these concepts, you can unlock the full potential of your leadership and drive your organization toward greater success, feeling equipped and empowered with the tools to rebuild PsyCap.

Rebuilding Psychological Capital

As any experienced leader knows, change doesn't happen overnight—and it does not happen without a concerted investment in employees' development and well-being. To shift the tide of negativity, leaders must go beyond surface-level interventions and tap into the deeper psychological resources that enable individuals and teams to thrive in the face of challenges and setbacks. This is not just a challenge, but also an opportunity for leaders to empower their teams and themselves, inspiring them to reach their full potential.

This is where the concept of psychological capital comes in. Coined by organizational behavior researchers Fred Luthans and Carolyn Youssef, psychological capital (or PsyCap) refers to "an individual's positive psychological state of development that is characterized by: (1) having confidence (self-efficacy) to take on and put in the necessary effort to succeed at challenging tasks; (2) making a positive attribution (optimism) about succeeding now and in the future; (3) persevering toward goals and, when necessary, redirecting paths to goals (hope) to succeed; and (4) when beset by problems and adversity, sustaining and bouncing back and even beyond (resilience) to attain success" (Luthans et al., 2007, p. 3).

> Cultivating psychological capital is not about forcing positivity, but equipping people with mental resources to respond constructively to challenges.

PsyCap is the mental toolkit that allows employees to navigate the ups and downs of work with a sense of agency, positivity, and adaptability. Moreover, as a growing body of research shows, it is a crucial driver of employee engagement, job satisfaction, and organizational performance (Avey et al., 2011; Newman et al., 2014).

Developing Self-Efficacy

The first component of PsyCap is self-efficacy: the belief in one's ability to accomplish tasks and achieve goals successfully. Employees with high self-efficacy are likelier to take on challenging projects, persist in facing obstacles, and bounce back from failures (Bandura, 1997).

One of the most effective ways to build self-efficacy is through mastery experiences—opportunities to accomplish tasks and build competence over time. As Aaron, a healthcare CEO, explained, "Our mid-level leaders have to take control and solve those things that are causing problems for our team members because that builds trust and confidence that they can take issues to that leader."

By empowering employees to take ownership of problems and develop solutions, leaders can help them build the confidence and skills to tackle increasingly complex challenges. This might involve:

* Providing opportunities for stretch assignments and professional development
* Breaking down significant goals into manageable sub-goals
* Offering regular feedback and coaching to support skill development
* Celebrating progress and accomplishments along the way

Another way to build self-efficacy is through social modeling—observing others complete tasks and achieve goals. As Bandura (1997) explains, seeing how others succeed can boost our confidence in our abilities, mainly when we identify their struggles and triumphs.

Leaders can leverage social modeling by:

* Sharing success stories and case studies from across the organization
* Pairing employees with mentors or role models who can provide guidance and support

* Encouraging peer-to-peer learning and knowledge sharing
* Publicly recognizing and celebrating team and individual achievements

By creating opportunities for mastery experiences and social modeling, leaders play a crucial role in helping employees build self-efficacy to confidently and skillfully take on even the toughest challenges. Your leadership is instrumental in this process.

Cultivating Optimism

The second component of PsyCap is optimism: the tendency to expect positive outcomes and attribute setbacks to temporary, external factors rather than permanent, personal deficiencies. When optimistic, employees are more likely to persist in adversity, maintain motivation and engagement, and contribute to a positive organizational climate (Seligman, 2011).

One way to cultivate optimism is through cognitive reframing. This technique helps employees shift from a pessimistic to an optimistic mindset. Mel described this process succinctly: "It's all about spiraling up in dialogue instead of spiraling down. People often prefer spiraling down because it feels easier." This approach encourages positive thinking patterns and can improve overall workplace attitudes. Leaders can encourage this kind of "spiraling up" by:

* Modeling optimistic language and behavior themselves
* Challenging negative self-talk and pessimistic attributions
* Encouraging employees to look for opportunities and lessons in setbacks
* Helping teams develop contingency plans and create proactive problem-solving strategies

Another way to build optimism is through gratitude practices - regularly reflecting on and expressing appreciation for the good things in one's work and life.

As Steve shared, "Gratitude, appreciation, kindness, all expressions of love are the anecdote for toxicity."

Leaders can incorporate gratitude into their teams' routines by:

* Starting meetings with a round of appreciation or "good news" sharing
* Encouraging employees to keep gratitude journals or share gratitude with colleagues
* Sending personalized thank-you notes or recognition for a job well done
* Celebrating team and organizational successes, big and small

Leaders can help employees maintain a positive outlook despite challenges and setbacks by intentionally cultivating a culture of optimism and gratitude.

Building Hope

The third component of PsyCap is hope: the ability to set meaningful goals, identify pathways to achieve those goals and maintain motivation. When employees are hopeful, they are more likely to take initiative, think creatively, and persevere in facing obstacles (Snyder, 2002).

One way to build hope is through goal-setting exercises that help employees clarify their aspirations, break them down into manageable steps, and develop contingency plans for overcoming barriers. As an education superintendent, Peter stated, "Every system is perfectly designed to produce the results it achieves." By intentionally creating goal-oriented systems that foster hope and agency, leaders can better support employees in reaching their objectives.

This might involve:

* Collaboratively setting SMART (specific, measurable, achievable, relevant, time-bound) goals
* Using "if-then" planning to anticipate and prepare for potential obstacles

* Providing regular feedback and coaching to support goal pursuit
* Celebrating milestones and progress along the way

Another way to cultivate hope is through autonomy support - giving employees the freedom and flexibility to approach their work in ways that align with their strengths, interests, and values. When employees feel a sense of ownership and control over their work, they are more likely to find meaning and motivation in even the most challenging tasks.

Leaders can support autonomy by:

* Involving employees in decision-making processes that affect their work
* Providing choice and flexibility in how work gets done
* Encouraging experimentation and innovation
* Trusting employees to manage their time and priorities effectively

By nurturing a sense of hope and autonomy, leaders can tap into employees' intrinsic motivation and creativity - key drivers of engagement and performance.

Fostering Resilience

The final component of PsyCap is resilience: the capacity to bounce back from adversity, learn from failures, and grow in the face of challenges. When employees are resilient, they can better adapt to change, cope with stress, and maintain their well-being and productivity over time (Southwick & Charney, 2012).

One way to foster resilience is through mindfulness training, which helps employees develop self-awareness and emotional regulation skills to navigate demanding situations with clarity and calmness. Leaders can incorporate mindfulness into their teams' routines by:

* Providing access to mindfulness apps, classes, or workshops
* Encouraging regular breaks and opportunities for reflection

* Modeling mindful communication and conflict resolution
* Creating a culture of psychological safety where it is okay to discuss challenges and setbacks

Another way to build resilience is through supportive relationships - fostering a sense of belonging, trust, and mutual support among team members. When employees feel connected to their colleagues and leaders, they are more likely to seek help, share knowledge and resources, and bounce back from setbacks more quickly (Carmeli et al., 2009).

Leaders can cultivate supportive relationships by:

* Creating opportunities for social connection and team building
* Modeling vulnerability and openness in their interactions
* Providing mentoring and coaching support
* Encouraging a culture of peer support and collaboration

By prioritizing mindfulness and supportive relationships - and equipping employees with the skills and resources needed to navigate challenges effectively - leaders can foster the resilience needed to thrive in an ever-changing world of work.

Creating a Supportive Environment

Of course, cultivating the four components of PsyCap—self-efficacy, optimism, hope, and resilience—requires more than just a toolkit of individual-level interventions. To deeply embed these psychological resources into the organization's fabric, leaders must also create a supportive environment that encourages learning, innovation, and growth.

This means fostering a culture of psychological safety where employees feel comfortable speaking up, sharing ideas, and taking risks without fear of punishment or embarrassment (Edmondson, 1999). It means providing continuous learning and development opportunities and making it safe to fail and try again.

Moreover, it means recognizing and rewarding employees for their successes, efforts, progress, and growth.

As Heather said brilliantly, "If you were hired here, you are worthy of being here. Furthermore, I believe that everyone is worthy to be included."

Conclusion

Cultivating PsyCap - self-efficacy, optimism, hope, and resilience - is a powerful way to unlock the potential of individuals and teams, even in the face of negative organizational cultures. Sarah's journey from a stressed, uncertain new executive to a confident, inspiring leader exemplifies the transformative power of developing these core psychological resources. By investing in PsyCap, leaders like Sarah can help employees build the mental strength and agility needed to navigate the challenges and opportunities of today's fast-paced, ever-changing world of work.

However, as Sarah's story illustrates, PsyCap is not a quick fix or a one-time initiative. It requires a sustained commitment to employee well-being and development embedded in the organization's everyday practices and norms. Sarah's ongoing work with her coach and her dedication to personal growth demonstrate the continuous nature of this process. It requires leaders who, like Sarah, are willing to model the qualities they seek to cultivate in others - who are authentic, emotionally intelligent, and growth-minded in their approach to leadership.

Moreover, Sarah's experience shows that cultivating PsyCap requires a fundamental shift in mindset—from focusing on deficits and problems to concentrating on strengths and possibilities. As Sarah learned to reframe challenges as opportunities and to approach setbacks with resilience, she created a ripple effect throughout her team and organization. By recognizing and amplifying the best in themselves and others, leaders can create a virtuous cycle of positivity, purpose, and

> Leaders who model and nurture psychological capital create a ripple effect of positivity throughout their organizations.

performance that transforms not just their
teams but also their organizations and communities.

So, as we continue on this journey of transforming negative workplace cultures, let us remember the power of PsyCap - and the role that each of us can play in nurturing it in ourselves and others. When we tap into the incredible resilience and potential of the human spirit, there is no limit to what we can achieve together. Whether facing market pressures, internal challenges, or personal doubts, cultivating PsyCap can provide the foundation for effective leadership and organizational success in even the most demanding circumstances.

Recap: Step 4 - Rebuild Psychological Capital

This chapter explored the importance of rebuilding psychological capital (PsyCap) in the workplace, focusing on its four key components: self-efficacy, optimism, hope, and resilience.

Key Insights:

* PsyCap is essential for individual and organizational success in challenging work environments.
* High PsyCap is associated with increased employee engagement and reduced burnout.
* Self-efficacy can be developed through mastery experiences and social modeling.
* Optimism can be rebuilt through cognitive reframing and gratitude practices.
* Hope is built through effective goal setting and autonomy support.
* Resilience is fostered through mindfulness training and supportive relationships.
* Creating a supportive environment with psychological safety is crucial for developing PsyCap.
* Cultivating PsyCap requires sustained commitment and a shift in mindset towards strengths and possibilities.

STEP 4 - REBUILD PSYCHOLOGICAL CAPITAL

5 Leadership Reflection Questions:

1. How am I currently modeling and supporting the development of self-efficacy in my team?

2. In what ways can I encourage more optimistic thinking and gratitude practices within my organization?

3. How effectively am I setting and communicating goals that inspire hope and motivation in my team?

4. What strategies am I using to foster resilience in myself and my team members?

5. How can I create a more supportive environment that encourages the development of PsyCap in my organization?

Team Discussion Exercise: PsyCap Strength Spotting

Objective: To practice recognizing and reinforcing PsyCap components in team interactions.

Materials: Notepads, pens, whiteboard, or flip chart

Instructions:

1. Introduce the four components of PsyCap (self-efficacy, optimism, hope, resilience) and provide brief definitions.

2. Divide the team into pairs.

3. Ask each pair to share a recent work challenge they faced and how they overcame it.

4. As partners share their stories, ask listeners to identify and note down examples of PsyCap components they hear in the story.

5. After both partners have shared, have them discuss the PsyCap components they identified in each other's stories.

6. Bring the full group back together and ask for volunteers to share examples of PsyCap they spotted in their partner's story.

7. Record these examples on a whiteboard, categorized by the four PsyCap components.

8. As a group, discuss:

- Which PsyCap components seem to be strengths in the team?
- Which components might need more development?
- How can the team leverage these strengths in future challenges?
- What strategies can the team use to further develop their PsyCap?

9. Conclude by having each team member share one action they'll take to rebuild a specific PsyCap component in the coming week.

This exercise helps team members recognize PsyCap in action, appreciate each other's strengths, and identify areas for further development. It also reinforces the idea that PsyCap is already present in the team and can be further cultivated.

Chapter 7
Step 5 - Address Negativity Constructively

As we explored in Chapter 1, the profound influence of the human brain's negativity bias on our perception and interpretation of the world cannot be overstated. This bias, deeply ingrained in our human development, has the power to shape our attitudes, behaviors, and interactions in the workplace, with far-reaching implications for organizational culture and performance.

Negativity bias, by its very nature, skews our perception of daily events, often leading us to disproportionately focus on what's going wrong rather than what is going right. A single criticism can cast a shadow over numerous praises, and one setback can overshadow numerous successes. This skewed perception can trigger a self-reinforcing spiral of negative attitudes and actions, underscoring the urgent need for intervention.

When left unchecked, these negative spirals can lead to destructive behaviors rather than constructive ones. Employees may become cynical, less engaged, and more prone to conflict. Leaders might make decisions based on fear rather than opportunity, stifling innovation, and growth. The result is a workplace environment where negativity becomes the norm, eroding morale, productivity, and engagement.

Moreover, in our interconnected modern workplaces, negativity can spread like wildfire. Bad news or negative attitudes can quickly propagate through an organization, affecting not just individuals or teams but entire departments or even the whole company. This wildfire effect can be particularly damaging during change or uncertainty when clear communication and strong leadership are crucial. Steve, a veteran CEO, candidly shared the challenges of leading through significant organizational change and the importance of persistence in the face of negativity: "As a CEO, I've learned that not everyone will support change, even when it's necessary. It's frustrating that we can't always get everyone fully committed to our goals. These days, there's less loyalty between companies and employees, which makes leading even harder. But we have to keep pushing forward anyway." Steve emphasizes the importance of addressing negativity directly and providing support before taking more drastic measures. He counsels leaders with his sage advice: "If someone's being negative, we'll try to help them. We'll listen, support, and offer coaching. But if nothing improves after a while, we might have to let them go."

> Addressing negativity constructively requires a balance of empathy, action, and solution-oriented thinking.

Just as negativity can spiral downward, positivity can spiral upward. The concept of 'spiraling up' captures the collective steps, informed by research, evaluation, and time-tested experience, for shifting the momentum from negative to positive, even amid challenging times. It involves intentional efforts to reframe perspectives, foster resilience, and cultivate a more balanced, constructive approach to workplace challenges. This concept is not just about countering negativity, but about actively promoting a positive and resilient culture in the workplace.

However, addressing negativity constructively remains one of the most significant challenges for leaders at all levels. It requires a delicate balance of empathy and action, acknowledging difficulties while maintaining forward momentum. Leaders must navigate the complex terrain of human emotions and organizational dynamics while steering their teams toward positive outcomes. Leader's need strategies for addressing negativity constructively, drawing on real-world experiences and evidence-based practices. We'll examine how leaders can recognize the signs of negativity, intervene effectively, and create environments where positive spirals can flourish.

Rightsize Up Institutional Banking

To illustrate these principles in action, let's consider the case of Mollie, a seasoned executive at an established financial institution. She had led her organization through a significant restructuring involving layoffs, an unprecedented task for the company deeply rooted in tradition and stability. Her experience offers valuable insights into the complexities of managing negativity during times of organizational upheaval. Despite the relatively small scale of the layoffs in terms of numbers, the impact on the organization's culture was profound. Mollie noted, "Numerically speaking, it was tiny, but the impact across the culture was huge."

In her approach to addressing the negativity, Mollie implemented several strategies that proved effective:

> 1. Immediate engagement is crucial in addressing negativity: Recognizing the signs of negativity, leaders must take swift action to engage with their teams. This can involve conducting check-ins with team leaders, spot-checks with trusted team members, and organizing all-staff team meetings.
> 2. Reinforcing organizational identity: Mollie focused on reminding the team of their organizational purpose and values, attempting to reconnect employees with the company's mission during uncertainty.
> 3. Open communication: She prioritized transparency and honest dialogue, creating spaces for employees to voice their concerns and feel reassured that their voices were heard. This open communication was a critical factor in addressing the resulting negativity. For instance, Mollie held regular town hall meetings where employees could ask questions and share their thoughts. She also set up a suggestion box system to encourage anonymous feedback, and she made a point to personally respond to each submission.

However, upon reflection, she also identified areas where her approach could have been improved:

1. Sustained engagement: she realized she had pulled back too quickly, especially with her direct reports leading the change. "I probably did not do enough of that for her," she admitted, referring to a VP struggling with the consolidation process.
2. Earlier strategic influence: She recognized the need to have more influence exerted earlier in the decision-making process, potentially shaping the communication strategy and implementation steps.
3. Longer evaluation period: she should have taken more time to deeply evaluate talent and understand potential frustrations before rushing to the "new end state."
4. Team building during transition: Mollie realized the importance of maintaining team cohesion during the change process. She reflected, underscoring the need for continuous team building during transitions.

This case study illustrates the critical importance of constructively addressing negativity during organizational change. It highlights the need for leaders to remain consistently engaged, balance empathy with forward momentum, and recognize the long-lasting impact that their actions can have on organizational trust and culture.

By learning from the successes and missteps of experienced leaders, we can develop more effective approaches to managing negativity and steering our organizations toward a more positive, resilient future. In Mollie's case study, we can compare traditional problem-based consultative models and Appreciative Inquiry methods, drawing from the research in your Stages of Consulting.

Mollie's experience highlights the challenges of addressing negativity in organizations, especially during significant change. While her approach incorporated elements of both problem-solving and strength-based strategies, it is worth examining how these different methodologies can shape our approach to organizational change and addressing negativity.

Many consultants and leaders have traditionally relied on problem-based approaches to address organizational issues. This method, rooted in logic and reason, identifies what is wrong and develops solutions to fix these problems. As noted in the research, problem-solving tends to emphasize "knowing" over "doing" (Allio, 2011; Block, 2011).

However, an alternative approach has gained traction recently: Appreciative Inquiry (AI). This strength-based methodology shifts the focus from what's wrong to what's working well, aiming to build momentum by investing energy in the organization's positive aspects.

> Appreciative Inquiry offers a powerful alternative to problem-based approaches by focusing on strengths and possibilities.

The critical difference between these approaches lies in their fundamental questions and focus:

Problem-Based Approach:
* Asks: "What problems are we facing?"
* Focuses on Identifying and fixing deficiencies
* Goal: Eliminate what is not working

Appreciative Inquiry:
* Asks: "What's working well that we can build upon?"
* Focuses on: Discovering and amplifying strengths
* Goal: Multiply what's already successful

Appreciative Inquiry employs a set of discovery questions designed to uncover and leverage organizational strengths:

1. Find observable exceptions - What's working well?
2. Interview interested participants - Who is interested in helping?
3. Identify positive deviants by invitation - Who's willing to partner?
4. Discover the "truth" - What have we learned?
5. Share the "truth" - What strategies multiply what's working?

This approach can be particularly effective in addressing negativity by redirecting focus and energy toward positive aspects of the organization. As David Cooperrider, one of the founders of AI, states: "Human systems grow in the direction of what they persistently ask questions about" (Cooperrider & McQuaid, 2012).

Research has shown the effectiveness of AI in various organizational contexts. For instance, a study by Gesser-Edelsburg et al. (2021) found that using a positive deviance approach in healthcare settings improved practices and outcomes. They noted that focusing on successful outliers and spreading their practices was more effective than traditional problem-solving approaches.

Moreover, organizations that have implemented AI have reported significant improvements. For example, Nutrients for Life Foundation reported a 300% increase in fundraising after implementing AI. In comparison, Green Mountain Coffee Roasters saw a 300% increase in stock price over two years following an AI summit (Cooperrider & McQuaid, 2012).

By shifting the focus from "what is wrong" to "what is possible," Appreciative Inquiry offers a powerful alternative for addressing negativity and driving positive organizational change. As leaders and consultants, understanding and applying both problem-based and strength-based approaches can provide a more comprehensive toolkit for addressing organizational challenges and fostering a more positive, resilient workplace culture.

Approaching Challenges with a Solution-Oriented Mindset

When faced with negativity in the workplace—whether it's an employee consistently underperforming, a team mired in conflict, or a project that has gone off the rails—it can be tempting to focus solely on the problem at hand. We might find ourselves dwelling on what's gone wrong, assigning blame, or feeling overwhelmed by the magnitude of the challenge.

However, as the executives I interviewed repeatedly emphasized, the most influential leaders approach negative situations with a solution-oriented mindset. Rather than getting bogged down in the problem, they focus their energy on finding a way forward, identifying the root causes and developing a plan of action to address them.

As Heather, a construction executive with over 20 years of experience, said, "Sometimes leaders have to make tough decisions that may seem harsh or unpopular in the short term. However, these decisions are often necessary and prove to be correct when viewed in the long run. Making these difficult choices can significantly impact the organization's future success, even if they're not well-received at first." In other words, influential leaders are willing to make difficult choices in the service of the greater good—to prioritize solutions over short-term comfort or popularity.

So, what does this look like in practice? Let us consider a real-life scenario. Imagine a team that consistently misses project deadlines. Instead of immediately assigning blame or making assumptions, a leader with a solution-oriented mindset might ask questions to better understand the perspectives and motivations of those involved. They might seek to identify the underlying needs or concerns driving the team's inability to meet deadlines and work collaboratively to address them. This might involve:

* Actively listening to employee concerns and feedback, even when it's difficult to hear
* Asking open-ended questions to gather more information and perspectives
* Reframing problems as opportunities for learning and growth
* Encouraging a culture of experimentation and calculated risk-taking

By approaching challenges with a spirit of curiosity and a focus on solutions, leaders can create an environment where negativity is seen not as a threat but as an opportunity for growth and improvement.

Providing Timely, Specific, and Constructive Feedback

Of course, not all negativity in the workplace can be solved through a simple reframing or a few probing questions. Sometimes, employees engage in behaviors or performance issues that require more direct feedback and intervention. In these situations, the key is for leaders to provide timely, specific, and constructive feedback. Rather than waiting for problems to fester or delivering vague criticisms, leaders play a crucial role in addressing issues head-on with clarity and care.

> Effective feedback should be timely, specific, constructive, and actionable.

As Peter, the education executive, shared, "When negativity isn't dealt with promptly, it tends to snowball. Ignoring the original problem not only fails to solve it, but also creates a new problem: the perception that issues aren't being addressed. This leads to a cycle where more negativity builds up over time." When leaders fail to provide timely feedback, they not only allow negative behaviors to continue - they also send a message that they don't care enough to intervene.

So, what does effective feedback look like? According to the Center for Creative Leadership (2021), it should be:

* Timely: Delivered as soon as possible after the behavior or issue occurs
* Specific: Focused on concrete actions or behaviors rather than vague generalities
* Constructive: Framed as an opportunity for growth and improvement rather than a personal attack
* Actionable: Accompanied by specific suggestions or steps for moving forward

For example, instead of telling an employee, "Your work has been sloppy lately," a leader might say, "I noticed that the last two reports you turned in had several errors in the data analysis section. Let's sit down and review the quality control process to see where we can improve."

By providing specific, actionable feedback delivered with care, leaders can help employees understand their strengths and areas for growth and feel motivated to make positive changes.

Facilitating Open Dialogue and Problem-Solving

Another critical strategy for constructively addressing negativity is facilitating open dialogue and collaborative problem-solving. When employees feel heard, respected, and empowered to contribute to solutions, they are more likely to engage positively with their work and colleagues.

One powerful technique for leaders to facilitate open dialogue is active listening—fully concentrating on, comprehending, responding to, and recalling what is being said (Robertson, 2005). When leaders listen actively to their employees, they send a message that their perspectives and experiences matter and that they are valued team members. Active listening involves:

> Facilitating open dialogue and collaborative problem-solving can transform negative situations into opportunities for growth.

* Giving the speaker your undivided attention
* Using nonverbal cues (e.g., eye contact, nodding) to show you are engaged
* Paraphrasing or summarizing what you've heard to ensure understanding
* Asking clarifying questions to gain more insight
* Withholding judgment or advice until the speaker has finished

Leaders can build trust, defuse tensions, and facilitate collaborative problem-solving by creating a safe space for employees to share their thoughts and concerns and demonstrating genuine interest and empathy.

This collaborative approach to addressing negativity is critical when dealing with interpersonal conflicts or team dynamics issues. Rather than trying to solve the problem unilaterally or imposing a solution from the above, effective leaders empower employees to work together to identify root causes and develop mutually satisfactory solutions.

As an education leader, Erica demonstrated a proactive approach to managing team dynamics and resolving conflicts saying "I intentionally observed the meetings. I intentionally met with the two of them together so that they could provide feedback to one another," she highlights the importance of active leadership in fostering open communication. This strategy allows team members to address issues directly, with the leader present to guide the conversation. Such an approach helps employees develop crucial conflict resolution skills and strengthens working relationships. By creating a structured environment for feedback and dialogue, leaders can transform potential conflicts into opportunities for growth and improved collaboration within the team.

Balancing Accountability with Support and Empathy

Even with the most skillful feedback and facilitation, there may be times when employees continue to engage in negative or counterproductive behaviors. In these situations, leaders must be willing to hold people accountable for their actions, set clear expectations and consequences, and follow through as needed. However, accountability doesn't have to mean punishment or blame. Instead, it can be an opportunity for growth and learning - helping employees take responsibility for their impact and make positive changes. The key is balancing accountability with support and empathy - approaching even the most challenging situations with a spirit of understanding and compassion. This means taking the time to understand the employee's perspective, offering resources and support to help them succeed, and framing the conversation around shared goals and values.

As Aaron, CEO, said, "I think of accountability as a love language. So, when I love people I care about, I will keep them accountable and surround them with resources for success. I can think of no better example of loving and caring for someone than setting high expectations and giving them the tools for success." This approach to accountability—one grounded in care and support rather than punishment—can be transformative for employees and teams alike. It sends a message that everyone is valued, that mistakes are growth opportunities, and that the organization is committed to helping people be their best selves.

> Balancing accountability with support and empathy is critical when addressing persistent negative behaviors.

Conclusion

Addressing negativity in the workplace is never easy - it requires skill, courage, and emotional intelligence. However, as Mollie's story and the other examples in this chapter demonstrate, it is also one of the most important things a leader can do to create a positive, productive, and psychologically healthy work environment. Mollie's experience with layoffs highlights the complexity of managing negativity during organizational change. Her initial approach, which combined immediate engagement, reinforcing organizational identity, and open communication, provided a solid foundation. However, her reflections on the need for sustained engagement, earlier strategic influence, and maintaining team cohesion during transition underscore the ongoing nature of addressing negativity constructively. Integrating Appreciative Inquiry (AI) into our approach to negativity can further enhance our effectiveness as leaders. Rather than solely focusing on problems, AI encourages us to identify and amplify what works well. This shift in perspective can be powerful in transforming negative situations into opportunities for growth and innovation.

By approaching negative situations with empathy, a solution-oriented mindset, and an appreciative lens, leaders can provide specific and constructive feedback, facilitate open dialogue and collaborative problem-solving, and balance accountability with support. This approach can transform even the most challenging dynamics into opportunities for growth and connection.

The goal is not to eliminate negativity - that would be impossible in any human system. Instead, it is to create a culture where negativity is addressed openly, constructively, and with care - where people feel safe to voice concerns, take risks, and learn from their mistakes. AI complements this goal by encouraging a focus on possibilities and strengths, even in the face of challenges.

As leaders, we have a profound opportunity and responsibility to model this constructive approach to negativity. By showing courage, compassion, and skill in even the most difficult moments and consistently seeking out and amplifying the positive, we can create a ripple effect of positivity that extends far beyond our teams and organizations. So, let us commit to the hard work of addressing negativity constructively approaching challenges with curiosity and grace, providing feedback with clarity and care, facilitating dialogue and collaboration, and holding ourselves and others accountable with love. Let us commit to consistently seeking out and building upon what's working well despite difficulties. Through this work, we can transform our workplaces—and our world—for the better, creating environments where individuals and organizations can thrive, even in the face of adversity.

Recap: Step 5 - Address Negativity Constructively

This chapter explored strategies for constructively addressing negativity in the workplace, drawing on real-world examples and evidence-based practices.

Key Insights:

* Negativity bias can skew perceptions and trigger self-reinforcing spirals of negative attitudes and actions.
* Addressing negativity constructively requires a balance of empathy, action, and

solution-oriented thinking.

* Immediate engagement, reinforcing organizational identity, and open communication are crucial when dealing with negativity during organizational change.

* Appreciative Inquiry offers a powerful alternative to problem-based approaches by focusing on strengths and possibilities.

* Effective feedback should be timely, specific, constructive, and actionable.

* Facilitating open dialogue and collaborative problem-solving can help transform negative situations into opportunities for growth.

* Balancing accountability with support and empathy is critical to addressing persistent negative behaviors.

5 Leadership Reflection Questions:

1. How do I typically respond to negativity in my organization? Am I more inclined towards problem-solving or strength-based approaches?

2. How can I improve my ability to provide timely, specific, and constructive feedback to my team members?

3. How effectively am I facilitating open dialogue and collaborative problem-solving in my team? What could I do to improve in this area?

4. How do I balance accountability with support and empathy when addressing persistent negative behaviors?

5. How might I incorporate Appreciative Inquiry principles into my leadership approach to address negativity more constructively?

Team Discussion Exercise: Reframing Negativity with Appreciative Inquiry

Objective: To practice reframing negative situations into opportunities for growth and positive change.

Materials: Whiteboard or flip chart, markers, sticky notes

Instructions:

1. Divide the team into small groups of 3-4 people.

2. Ask each group to identify a recent negative situation or challenge the team or organization has faced and write it on a sticky note.

3. Have groups place their sticky notes on a shared board.

4. For each situation, have the groups work together to:

a) Identify the negative aspects or impacts of the situation

b) Reframe the situation using Appreciative Inquiry principles, focusing on strengths and opportunities

c) Develop three specific, actionable steps to address the situation constructively

5. Have each group present their reframes and action steps to the team.

6. As a whole group, discuss:

• Which reframes were most impactful or surprising?

• How might adopting these reframed perspectives change how the team approaches challenges?

• What strategies can the team use to practice constructive approaches to negativity more regularly?

7. To conclude, have each team member share one insight they gained from the exercise and one action they commit to taking to address negativity more constructively in their work.

This exercise helps teams practice reframing negative situations, encourages collaborative problem-solving, and promotes a more constructive approach to workplace challenges.

Chapter 8
Step 6 - Leverage Positivity and Celebrate Success

As we've explored throughout *Spiraling Up*, creating a positive workplace culture is an ongoing process that requires consistent effort and attention from leaders at all levels. In this last step of our framework, we focus on the transformative power of reinforcing positivity and celebrating success. These actions can help solidify cultural changes and create a self-sustaining cycle of positivity within organizations, inspiring leaders to make a difference in their workplaces. To illustrate the transformative power of these practices, let's delve into Melanie's experiences as the Chief People Officer at a 100-year-old senior care organization. Melanie's approach to leadership and culture-building offers a compelling example of how reinforcing positivity and celebrating success can revolutionize an organization. When Melanie joined her organization, she made it her mission to shift the Culture toward gratitude, appreciation, and positivity. She understood that language and behavior were critical drivers of Culture, and she set out to change both through a series of intentional practices:

>1. *Personal Thank You Notes*: Melanie began writing handwritten thank you notes to employees' homes, recognizing their contributions and impact. As she puts it, "When they open it at their home, their families are seeing it, their kids are seeing it, and it speaks to the fact that that person made a difference."
>2. *Gratitude Practices*: Melanie introduced gratitude sharing in leadership huddles. What started as one or two submissions grew into pages of gratitude shared across the organization. She ex-

plains, "The more you see gratitude, the more your neural pathways change, that you see more gratitude, and that gives you the capacity when things are not going well to support and manage through difficulty."

3. *Celebrating Real Stories*: Instead of using stock photos, Melanie's team displayed actual employees in their social media posts, celebrating their aspirations and contributions. This practice helped to leverage the value of everyone's work and inspire others.

4. *Reframing Language*: Melanie actively shifted the language used in the organization. For example, she challenged the use of the term' human capital', a term often used to refer to employees as assets or resources, and insisted on more respectful, people-centered language. She believed using terms like 'team members' or 'colleagues' instead of 'human capital' would foster a more positive and respectful work environment.

5. *Personal Engagement*: Melanie committed to meeting with every team member annually for a structured interview and sharing what she learned. She also sent weekly messages to her team, maintaining consistent positive communication. This distinctive touch made each team member feel valued and connected, fostering a sense of belonging and positivity, instilling a sense of empathy in leaders toward their team members.

The impact of these practices was significant. Despite joining an organization with a traditional culture, Melanie saw a dramatic shift over time. She observed people spontaneously expressing gratitude, sending thank you notes, and reframing negative situations into opportunities. Even in challenging conditions, such as a significant acquisition, Melanie's team's commitment to positivity and personal engagement made a significant difference. For instance, the number of thank you notes sent increased by 50% in the first year of Melanie's leadership, and using more respectful language became a norm in the organization.

As Melanie reflects, "You don't do the work because you think it's magically everything's going to be perfect. You do the work because it might make a difference for one or two or three people." Yet, over time, these small actions created a ripple effect throughout the organization, gradually transforming the Culture. This ripple effect demonstrates the significant role of each leader in shaping a positive workplace culture, making them feel responsible and empowered.

> Reinforcing positivity and celebrating success are not just feel-good exercises - they are powerful tools for cultural transformation.

Melanie's experience demonstrates that reinforcing positivity and celebrating success are not just feel-good exercises - they are powerful tools for cultural transformation. By consistently focusing on the joyous moments, expressing gratitude, and celebrating individual and collective achievements, leaders can create an environment where positivity becomes self-reinforcing, and negativity finds less fertile ground.

Positivity Culture by the numbers

Melanie's success story demonstrates simple practices, but few organizations actually implement her approach. The COVID-19 pandemic has highlighted the importance of positive workplace cultures. It has also sharpened the contrast between organizations that prioritize positivity and those that don't. This divide has become increasingly apparent in the wake of the global health crisis, underscoring the critical role of a positive work environment in today's business landscape.

A 2022 global study by McKinsey & Company revealed that companies focusing on employee well-being and positive workplace culture during the pandemic outperformed their peers significantly. These companies experienced 23% higher profitability, 18% higher productivity, and a remarkable 66% lower turnover rate than organizations that neglected these aspects.

The study found that organizations prioritizing positivity and employee recognition were better equipped to handle the challenges posed by the pandemic. They showed greater adaptability in transitioning to remote work, maintained higher levels of employee engagement, and demonstrated more resilience in economic uncertainty. In contrast, organizations with negative cultures that failed to acknowledge employee contributions faced severe consequences. A survey conducted by the Society for Human Resource Management (SHRM) in early 2023 found that in companies characterized by negativity and lack of recognition, 68% of employees reported feeling disengaged, 73% were actively looking for new jobs, and productivity had dropped by an average of 29%. These statistics show that reinforcing positivity and celebrating success are not just feel-good exercises. They are critical strategies that directly impact an organization's bottom line and ability to navigate challenging times.

Companies focusing on employee well-being and positive workplace culture during the pandemic outperformed their peers by 23% in profitability.

Take, for example, the contrasting experiences of two mid-sized tech companies during the pandemic I consulted with; a SAAS-based tech company, which had a long-standing tradition of celebrating employee successes and fostering a positive work environment, smoothly transitioned to remote work. They maintained weekly virtual "win" meetings, implemented a digital peer-to-peer recognition platform, and organized virtual team-building events. As a result, they saw a 15% increase in productivity and a 95% employee retention rate and even managed to grow their business by 20% during the pandemic. However, a financial firm that had always prioritized results over employee well-being struggled. Their top-down, high-pressure Culture translated poorly to remote work. With no systems in place for recognition or positive reinforcement, employee morale plummeted. They experienced a 40% turnover rate, a 25% drop in productivity, and saw their market share shrink by 30%.

These contrasting examples highlight a crucial point: reinforcing positivity and celebrating success are essential. They're about creating an environment where people can bring their whole selves to work, feel valued and supported, and are empowered to do their best work. In such an environment, innovation flourishes, productivity soars, and organizations become more resilient in the face of challenges.

Why Leaders Don't Celebrate

Despite the clear benefits of recognition and celebration, many organizations need help making them a consistent part of their Culture. Understanding the barriers that prevent leaders from celebrating is crucial to overcoming them.

Consider the case of Alex, the CEO of a rapidly growing tech startup. Under Alex's leadership, the company achieved impressive milestones, but the workplace culture needed to be more positive. Alex prided himself on his "no-nonsense" approach, believing that hard work should be its reward. He saw the celebration as a waste of time and resources, often saying, "We're not here to throw parties; we're here to build a business."

This mindset trickled down through the organization. Emulating Alex's style, department heads rarely acknowledged their teams' achievements. Sensing that the celebration wasn't valued, middle managers focused solely on hitting targets. Employees, feeling unappreciated, became increasingly disengaged.

The impact was significant. Despite the company's financial success, turnover rates were high, and innovation had stagnated. Team members worked in silos, reluctant to share ideas or collaborate. The once-vibrant startup was turning into a cold, impersonal workplace.

Alex's approach exemplifies several common barriers that prevent leaders from celebrating:

> 1. Fear of appearing unprofessional: Some leaders worry that too much celebration might undermine their authority or make the workplace seem less severe.
> 2. Concern about setting unrealistic expectations: There's a fear

that celebrating successes might set a precedent that's hard to maintain or lead to complacency.

3. Time constraints and competing priorities: In the rush of daily business, celebration often falls to the bottom of the to-do list.

4. Discomfort with emotional expression: Some leaders feel awkward or vulnerable expressing appreciation or leading celebrations.

5. Cultural factors: Public praise or celebration may be inappropriate or unnecessary in some organizational or national cultures.

6. Results-oriented mindset: Leaders may focus solely on outcomes, overlooking the importance of recognizing effort and progress.

7. Lack of awareness: Some leaders need to realize the impact of celebration and recognition on employee motivation and performance.

Overcoming these barriers requires a fundamental shift in mindset. Leaders must recognize that celebration and recognition are not "nice-to-haves" but essential components of a high-performing culture. By reframing celebration as a strategic tool for motivation and engagement, leaders can prioritize it alongside other critical business activities.

> Recognition and celebration play a crucial role in empowering positivity champions within the organization.

This shift in perspective is crucial because reinforcing positivity goes beyond simple recognition. It's about creating an environment where employees feel valued, supported, and empowered to do their best work. It's about fostering a sense of belonging and purpose that transcends the day-to-day tasks of the job.

As leaders, it's time to challenge ourselves. Take a moment to reflect on your leadership practices. How often do you celebrate your team's achievements? Do you make a conscious effort to recognize individual contributions? Or do you find yourself falling into the same patterns as Alex, constantly pushing for the next goal without pausing to appreciate the journey?

Consider celebration not just a discipline or practice but a fundamental shift in how we view and value our people. It's about recognizing that our team members are not just resources to be utilized but human beings with intrinsic worth whose efforts and achievements deserve acknowledgment.

Look around your organization. Are there leaders or team members who excel at celebrating and appreciating others? These individuals can serve as powerful role models. Observe their practices, learn from their approach, and find ways to emulate their positive behaviors.

Remember, the goal isn't to replicate someone else's style exactly but to develop your authentic way of showing appreciation and celebrating success. It might initially feel uncomfortable, especially if it's not your natural inclination. But with practice, it can become an integral part of your leadership style.

As you move forward, challenge yourself to find at least one thing to celebrate daily. It doesn't have to be grand or elaborate - a simple word of thanks, a brief email of appreciation, or a moment of recognition in a team meeting can make a significant difference. By consistently reinforcing positivity and celebrating success, you can transform your team's Culture, one interaction at a time.

The Power of Fun in the Workplace

Imagine entering an office where laughter echoes through the halls, colleagues greet each other with genuine smiles, and the air buzzes with creative energy. This isn't a fantasy – it's the reality of workplaces that have embraced the power of fun. As Catherine Price eloquently puts it in her book "The Power of Fun: How to Feel Alive Again," actual fun emerges at the intersection of playfulness, connection, and flow. Let's explore how these elements can transform the daily grind into a fulfilling journey.

Playfulness: Where Innovation Thrives

Picture Emma, a software developer at a bustling tech startup. She dreaded Monday mornings, but that changed when her company introduced "Wacky Idea Wednesdays." Now, she looks forward to these midweek brainstorming sessions where no idea is too outlandish.

Last Wednesday, Emma's team was tasked with reimagining their product's user interface. Instead of a traditional meeting, they engaged in a playful exercise: each team member had to draw their ideal interface while blindfolded, resulting in hilarious sketches and unexpected insights. As they laughed over their artistic attempts, Emma had a eureka moment. The simplicity of her blindfolded design sparked an idea for a streamlined, intuitive interface that would later become a key feature of their product.

> The power of fun in the workplace emerges at the intersection of playfulness, connection, and flow.

This playful approach didn't just make work more enjoyable; it unlocked creativity that might have remained dormant in a more serious setting. As Dr. Stuart Brown, author of "Play: How it Shapes the Brain, Opens the Imagination, and Invigorates the Soul," would attest, play increases cognitive flexibility, making it easier to think outside the box and adapt to new challenges.

Connection: The Heart of Collaboration

Let's focus on Alex, a marketing manager recently joining a large corporation. Initially, Alex felt lost in the sea of unfamiliar faces, struggling to build relationships in the fast-paced environment. That changed when the company introduced a peer mentorship program.

Alex was paired with Samantha from the sales department. Their weekly coffee chats started as formal check-ins but soon became genuine friendships. They shared stories about their weekends, discussed industry trends, and even discovered a shared passion for rock climbing. This connection extended beyond their one-on-one interactions; Alex was more comfortable contacting colleagues, fostering a network of support and collaboration across departments.

The impact was profound. When Alex needed insights from sales for a crucial marketing campaign, he didn't hesitate to ask Samantha for help. Their collaboration resulted in a campaign that resonated deeply with customers, highlighting the power of cross-departmental teamwork.

This story exemplifies Simon Sinek's assertion in "Leaders Eat Last" that "the sense of belonging and connection in a team fosters trust and cooperation." By nurturing these connections, organizations create a tapestry of relationships that strengthen the entire company fabric.

Flow: Where Time Flies and Productivity Soars

Lastly, let's consider Maya, a data analyst who often found herself distracted by the constant ping of emails and impromptu meetings. Her work, which required deep concentration, was suffering. Everything changed when her company implemented "Flow Fridays."

On these days, Maya's calendar is cleared of meetings. She settles into a comfortable "focus pod" – a quiet, ergonomically designed space that minimizes distractions. As she dives into her data analysis, the outside world fades away. Hours pass unnoticed as Maya loses herself, uncovering patterns and insights into the numbers.

Maya emerges from her flow state, surprised to find the office empty. She realizes she's progressed more in one focused day than a distracted week. More importantly, she feels a deep sense of satisfaction and accomplishment. This flow experience, as described by Mihaly Csikszentmihalyi, is "the secret to happiness at work." Organizations boost productivity and enhance job satisfaction and personal fulfillment by creating conditions that allow employees to achieve this state of deep engagement.

The Ripple Effect of Fun

As these stories illustrate, the organizational Culture transforms when playfulness, connection, and flow become integral parts of the workday. Employees like Emma, Alex, and Maya don't just complete tasks; they innovate, collaborate, and find deep engagement in their work. They're not just counting down the hours but actively contributing to a vibrant, productive community. The smiles on their faces, the energy in their interactions, and the pride in their accomplishments are a testament to the power of fun in the workplace. It's not about frivolity; it's about creating an environment where people can bring their whole selves to work, where creativity flourishes, relationships thrive, and individuals can lose themselves in meaningful challenges.

So, as you reflect on your workplace, ask yourself: When was the last time you and your team experienced this kind of fun? Remember, the most telling metric of your progress in fostering a positive, thriving work environment isn't found in spreadsheets – it's written on the faces of your people. Their smiles, laughter, and expressions of engagement and fulfillment are the proper measures of a workplace where fun and success go hand in hand.

As we've seen, infusing fun into the workplace can dramatically transform organizational Culture. But fun is just one piece of the puzzle. Leaders must also model positive behaviors, recognize achievements, and provide ongoing support to create a thriving, positive work environment. Let's explore how these elements work together to leverage positivity and celebrate success in your organization.

Modeling and Reinforcing Positive Behaviors

The power of example cannot be overstated when it comes to shaping organizational Culture. Leaders who consistently model positive behaviors create a ripple effect throughout their teams, influencing how people think, feel, and interact. This role modeling can transform the entire workplace atmosphere. By consistently treating people with respect and compassion, leaders can create a sense of psychological safety that allows positive behaviors to flourish.

Of course, modeling positivity isn't always easy, especially in facing challenges. It requires a high degree of self-awareness, emotional intelligence, and self-regulation. Leaders must be willing to acknowledge mistakes, seek diverse perspectives, and continuously develop their positive psychological resources. For instance, when dealing with a difficult employee, a leader might need to consciously remain calm, empathize with the employee's perspective, and focus on finding constructive solutions.

The impact of this intentional modeling is significant. Research by Kim Cameron (2012) found that when leaders display positive behaviors such as gratitude, forgiveness, and kindness, it increases employee well-being, job satisfaction, and organizational commitment. A study published in the Journal of Applied Psychology revealed that positive leadership behaviors can improve team performance by up to 30%.

Leaders can employ various strategies to reinforce positive behaviors. They might regularly share stories of positive behaviors in action, publicly recognize employees who demonstrate these behaviors or provide opportunities for employees to practice and develop positive skills. Encouraging a culture of feedback and continuous improvement while holding everyone accountable to high standards of positivity and respect can create a "positivity flywheel" – a virtuous cycle that builds momentum over time.

Recognizing Achievements and Contributions

While modeling positive behaviors sets the tone, recognizing and celebrating achievements keeps the positivity engine running. Feeling seen, valued, and appreciated for their hard work can motivate employees, boosting engagement, loyalty, and a sense of belonging.

Darin emphasized the importance of intentionality in recognition: "Leading by example alone doesn't do it. Many people rely on that, like, 'Well, if they work with me, that'll work. They'll absorb it.' But that alone doesn't do it. You must be intentional about it. This underscores that recognition and celebration require deliberate effort and planning from leaders.

The impact of recognition on employee engagement is substantial. Gallup's research (2016) found that employees who receive regular recognition are up to six times more likely to be engaged than those who don't. Moreover, a study by Deloitte revealed that organizations with recognition programs have 31% lower voluntary turnover rates.

Effective recognition should be timely, specific, personalized, meaningful, and equitable. Leaders can incorporate recognition into their teams' routines in many ways. They might start meetings with a round of "shout-outs" or send personalized thank-you notes to employees. Providing opportunities for peer-to-peer recognition can also be powerful. A study by SHRM found that peer-to-peer recognition is 35.7% more likely to impact financial results than manager-only recognition positively.

Celebrating milestones and successes at both team and organizational levels is equally important. Whether completing a significant project, reaching a sales target, or marking an employee's work anniversary, these celebrations reinforce the value of hard work and dedication. According to a survey by Achievers, 93% of employees who feel valued by their employer are motivated to do their best work.

Sustaining Momentum Through Ongoing Support and Resources

Reinforcing positivity and celebrating success isn't a one-time event – it requires ongoing leadership support and resources. This is particularly crucial when sustaining gains in addressing negativity and transforming workplace culture.

Peter, an education superintendent, shared a valuable insight: "Negativity is a valuable source of information, revealing crucial insights into how people perceive and respond to your leadership and the services you provide." By viewing challenges as opportunities for growth and continuing to invest in employee well-being and development, leaders can ensure their organizations are well-equipped to handle future challenges and opportunities. Ongoing support and resourcing include:

* Providing access to training and development opportunities.
* Offering employee assistance programs.
* Regularly seeking out employee feedback.

Melanie, CPO, emphasized the foundational nature of this work: "Culture is both pervasive and fundamental to an organization. It's difficult to define precisely because it influences everything we do, like an umbrella covering all aspects of our work. At the same time, culture forms the foundation upon which the entire organization is built. It shapes our values, behaviors, and decision-making processes at every level."

The impact of this ongoing support is evident. According to a study by the American Psychological Association, 89% of workers at companies that support well-being initiatives are more likely to recommend their company as an excellent workplace. Furthermore, research by IBM found that companies that offer comprehensive training programs have 218% higher engagement per employee than those with less comprehensive programs.

Investing in tools and technologies that facilitate collaboration and innovation can also be crucial. A study by McKinsey found that companies that use social technologies can increase the productivity of high-skill knowledge workers by 20-25%. Similarly, providing competitive compensation and benefits packages shows employees they are valued and supported. A survey by Glassdoor found that 63% of job seekers look at salary and compensation before other factors when considering a job offer.

> Embedding positivity into organizational DNA requires constant attention and reinforcement across all aspects of operations.

Reinforcing positivity and celebrating success is not just a nice-to-have – it's a fundamental part of creating a workplace where people can thrive. By consistently modeling positive behaviors, recognizing achievements, and providing ongoing support and resources, leaders can develop a culture of positivity that drives engagement, productivity, and overall organizational success. The statistics speak for themselves: organizations prioritizing these elements significantly improve employee satisfaction, retention, and performance. As you reflect on your leadership practices, consider how you can incorporate these strategies to reinforce positivity and celebrate success in your organization.

Conclusion

As we conclude our exploration of *Spiraling Up*, it's clear that reinforcing positivity and celebrating success are not merely optional extras in the workplace - they are essential components of a thriving, resilient organizational culture. Throughout this journey, we've seen how leaders like Melanie have transformed their organizations through intentional practices of gratitude, recognition, and personal engagement. We've examined the stark contrasts between companies prioritizing positivity and those not, particularly in challenging times like the COVID-19 pandemic.

The power of fun in the workplace, as illustrated through the experiences of Emma, Alex, and Maya, demonstrates how playfulness, connection, and flow can revolutionize our work environments. These elements make work more enjoyable and drive innovation, collaboration, and productivity.

We've also confronted the barriers that often prevent leaders from celebrating, as exemplified by Alex's "no-nonsense" approach, and explored strategies to overcome these obstacles. The research is clear: organizations prioritizing positivity and employee recognition outperform their peers in profitability, productivity, and employee retention.

Moreover, we've delved into the crucial roles of modeling positive behaviors, recognizing achievements, and providing ongoing support and resources. Leaders like Heather and Darin have shown us the transformative power of intentional, positive leadership. The statistics speak volumes - from increased employee engagement to lower turnover rates, the benefits of a positive workplace culture are undeniable.

As we close this chapter, it's important to remember that creating and maintaining a positive workplace culture is an ongoing journey, not a destination. It requires consistent effort, intentionality, and commitment from all leaders.

Recap: Step 6 - Leverage Positivity and Celebrate Success

This chapter explored the importance of cultivating psychological capital (PsyCap) in the workplace, focusing on its four key components: self-efficacy, optimism, hope, and resilience.

Key Insights:

* Reinforcing positivity and celebrating success is crucial for solidifying cultural changes and creating a self-sustaining cycle of positivity within organizations.
* Personal engagement, gratitude practices, and celebrating real stories can significantly impact organizational Culture, as demonstrated by Melanie's experience as Chief People Officer.
* Companies focusing on employee well-being and a positive workplace culture outperform their peers in profitability, productivity, and employee retention.
* Fun in the workplace, characterized by playfulness, connection, and flow, can boost innovation, collaboration, and overall job satisfaction.
* Leaders must consistently model positive behaviors to create a ripple effect throughout their teams.
* Recognition and celebration of achievements are vital for maintaining employee motivation and engagement.
* Ongoing support and resources are essential for sustaining positive cultural changes over time.

> **Leadership Reflection Questions:**
>
> 1. How often do I actively leverage positivity and celebrate successes within my team or organization?
>
> 2. How can I incorporate more playfulness, connection, and opportunities for flow in our workplace?
>
> 3. What barriers prevent me from celebrating more frequently, and how can I overcome them?
>
> 4. How can I improve my approach to recognizing and appreciating individual and team contributions?
>
> 5. What additional resources or support can I provide to sustain positive cultural changes in my organization?

Challenge to Leaders:

As you reflect on your leadership practices, I challenge you to take concrete steps toward reinforcing positivity and celebrating success in your organization. Start by identifying one area where you can make an immediate impact. It could be implementing a weekly gratitude practice in your team meetings or creating a peer-to-peer recognition program. It could be redesigning a workspace to encourage flow or introducing a playful element to your problem-solving processes.

Whatever you choose, commit to it for the next 30 days. Document the changes you observe in your team's morale, productivity, and overall workplace atmosphere. Please share your experiences with your peers and encourage them to join you in this positivity challenge.

Remember, Melanie insightfully observed, "The motivation for doing meaningful work isn't the expectation of achieving perfection. Instead, it's the potential to positively impact even a few individuals." This perspective highlights that significant change often starts small. While the immediate effects may seem limited, these efforts can set in motion a chain reaction, gradually influencing and reshaping the culture and dynamics of entire organizations.

The most powerful metric of your progress won't be found in spreadsheets or quarterly reports. It will be written on the faces of your team members—in their smiles, energy, engagement, and fulfillment. As you embark on this journey, keep your eyes open for these signs. They accurately measure a workplace where positivity thrives, and success is celebrated.

By accepting this challenge, you're improving your workplace and contributing to a broader movement towards more human-centered, positive organizations. You're creating an environment where people can bring their whole selves to work, where creativity flourishes, relationships thrive, and individuals can lose themselves in meaningful challenges.

The journey of reinforcing positivity and celebrating success starts with you today.

Team Exercise: Fun-Powered Positivity Boost

Objective: To create a plan for reinforcing positivity and celebrating success using the elements of playfulness, connection, and flow.

Instructions:

1. Playful Warm-up (10 minutes): Start with a quick, playful icebreaker. For example, have everyone share their name and an imaginary superpower they'd use to make work more fun.

2. Connection Circles (20 minutes):

   - Form small groups of 3-4 people, ensuring a mix of departments.

   - In these groups, each person should share a recent work success and how it made them feel.

   - Group members respond by sharing how that person's success positively impacted them or the team.

3. Flow-State Brainstorming (30 minutes):

   - Provide large sheets of paper and colorful markers to each group.

   - Set a timer for 20 minutes of uninterrupted brainstorming.

   - Task: Create a "Celebration and Positivity Reinforcement Plan" incorporating playfulness, connection, and flow elements.

   - Encourage wild ideas and visual representations.

4. Playful Presentations (20 minutes):

   - Each group presents their ideas in a fun, creative way (e.g., as a skit, song, or game show).

   - Other teams can add ideas in real time, fostering collaborative creativity.

5. Connection Voting (10 minutes):

    - Everyone gets three "fun tokens" (could be colorful stickers or even candy).

    - Participants place their tokens on the ideas they like best, moving around the room and chatting with others about the concepts.

6. Flow Action Planning (20 minutes):

    - Based on the voting, select the top ideas.

    - As a group, discuss how to implement these ideas, ensuring they maintain playfulness, connection, and flow.

    - Assign "Fun Champions" to lead each initiative.

7. Celebration Finale (10 minutes):

    - End the session with a quick, fun celebration of the work done.

    - This could be a group dance, a silly photo booth moment, or a "gratitude wave" where each person shares one thing, they're grateful for about the team.

Follow-up: Schedule a "Fun Check-In" in a month to review the implementation of ideas and their impact on positivity and celebration in the workplace. Encourage ongoing sharing of fun moments and successes between meetings.

This exercise not only plans for future celebration and positive reinforcement but also immediately implements the principles of fun, creating a memorable and engaging experience for the team.

PART 3: Putting It All Together

SPIRALING UP

Chapter 9
Leading the Transformation - A Holistic Approach

TRANSFORMING AN ORGANIZATION'S CULTURE from negativity to positivity requires a holistic, sustained effort led from the top. As the research and executive interviews conducted for my dissertation revealed, negativity bias can become deeply entrenched in workplace norms, attitudes, and behaviors if left unchecked. However, by taking an intentional, systematic approach grounded in authentic leadership principles, executives can shift their organizational culture in a more positive direction over time. This chapter outlines how to implement the SPIRAL 6-step framework developed through this study, to navigate everyday challenges, and measure progress in cultural transformation efforts.

Integrating the SPIRAL 6-Step Framework into Leadership Practice

The SPIRAL framework that emerged from this study provides a roadmap for executives to lead cultural transformation:

1. Strengthen Authentic Leadership: TRIBE
2. Pinpoint Negativity's Impact
3. Inspire Mindsets and Expectations
4. Rebuild Psychological Capital
5. Address Negativity Constructively
6. Leverage Positivity and Celebrate Success

While these steps are presented sequentially, it's important to note that they are often implemented in parallel and revisited cyclically as the transformation effort progresses. This flexibility ensures that the process can adapt to the changing needs of the organization. The key is to approach cultural change holistically, recognizing how each element reinforces the others.

Step 1: Strengthen Authentic Leadership

Authentic leadership forms the foundation for cultural transformation. One executive interviewed said, "Trust forms the foundation of respect, and respect is essential for maintaining a strong relationship. When trust erodes, respect follows, and the entire relationship can crumble as a result." (Carolyn). Authentic leaders build trust through consistent alignment between words and actions, transparency about challenges and mistakes, and genuine care for employees' well-being. This provides psychological safety for employees to voice concerns constructively and take risks in service of positive change.

> Authentic leadership forms the foundation for cultural transformation, building trust through consistent alignment of words and actions.

In my consulting work, I have observed how quickly employees notice disconnects between a leader's stated values and actual behaviors. One manufacturing CEO talked extensively about work-life balance but routinely sent emails at 2 AM and expected immediate responses. This eroded trust and reinforced a culture of stress and burnout. In contrast, a tech company founder I worked with modeled work-life boundaries by limiting her work hours and encouraging employees to fully disconnect on weekends and vacations. This consistent example did more to shift norms than any formal policy could have.

Strengthening authentic leadership starts with deep self-reflection. Executives must examine their biases, fears, and motivations that may unconsciously shape their leadership approach. 360-degree feedback, personality assessments, and executive coaching can offer valuable insights. Leaders must cultivate greater self-awareness, noticing their reactions and responding thoughtfully rather than reactively. Regular practices like journaling, meditation, or working with a coach help develop this ability over time.

And remember, the reason for authentic leadership is to create a positive, engaged, and high-performing organizational culture, and it starts with your TRIBE:

* Transparency: Open communication and honesty
* Reflection: Self-awareness and continuous personal growth
* Integrity: Ethical decision-making and moral courage
* Balance: Objective analysis and consideration of diverse perspectives
* Empowerment: Enabling others to succeed and reach their potential

Step 2: Pinpoint Negativity's Impact

Before cultural transformation can begin in earnest, leaders need to understand clearly how negativity is currently showing up and impacting the organization. As Darin noted, "When negative behavior goes unchecked in a company, it tends to grow and spread. Over time, this unchallenged negativity can become so ingrained that new employees, especially younger ones, start to view it as normal and acceptable. They might even think it's just how things are supposed to be in the workplace."

Pinpointing negativity's impact requires gathering both quantitative and qualitative data. Employee engagement surveys, turnover metrics, productivity data, and customer satisfaction scores can offer a high-level view. However, these need to be complemented by focus groups, one-on-one conversations, and observational data to understand employees' lived experiences. Leaders should look for signs of negativity, such as chronic complaining, blaming, defensiveness, apathy, and passive-aggressive behavior. For instance, a leader might notice a pattern of employees avoiding difficult conversations, which could indicate a fear of conflict and a negative culture.

Examining how organizational systems, processes, and norms may inadvertently reinforce negativity is essential. For instance, performance review processes that overemphasize criticism, rigid hierarchies that stifle innovation, or incentive structures that pit employees against each other. One retail company I consulted with had a long-standing practice of publicly calling out individual cashiers' metrics in daily huddles. While intended to motivate improvement, this practice created a culture of anxiety and resentment. Pinpointing negativity's impact also means acknowledging one's role in perpetuating it. Leaders must be willing to receive feedback on how their words, actions, or decisions may contribute to a negative climate. This requires humility and a growth mindset. As Peter shared, "When someone makes a mistake - no matter their job or level - they want two things: for their error to be recognized, and a chance to improve. This is true whether you're a waiter, an athlete, or a company leader."

Step 3: Inspire Positive Mindsets

With a clear picture of the current state, leaders can begin to inspire their people towards a compelling vision for a more positive future. This involves reframing how people think about work, relationships, and organizational challenges. The goal is to shift from a scarcity mindset focused on problems and limitations to an abundance mindset concentrating on possibilities and strengths. An abundance mindset is about seeing opportunities instead of obstacles, focusing on what can be done rather than what can't, and believing that there is enough for everyone. It's a shift from a 'glass half empty' to a 'glass half full' perspective.

Inspiring starts with leaders' language and attitude. Mel captures the essence of the book when she shared, "It is all about the spiraling up of the dialogue versus the spiraling down." This means consciously looking for and highlighting what works well, reframing setbacks as learning opportunities, and approaching challenges with curiosity rather than blame. Over time, this positive orientation becomes contagious, lifting the overall tone of workplace interactions. Setting clear expectations around positivity is also crucial. This does not mean suppressing all negative emotions or feedback but establishing norms for how concerns are raised and addressed constructively. One healthcare organization I worked with implemented a simple rule: for every problem raised in meetings, people had to suggest at least one potential solution. This slight shift sparked much more generative discussions.

Reframing also involves helping employees connect their day-to-day work to a larger sense of purpose and impact. People are much more likely to maintain a positive outlook when they understand how their efforts contribute to meaningful outcomes. For instance, a software company I consulted with started inviting customers to share stories of how the product improved their lives at all-hands meetings. Stories dramatically increased employees' sense of pride and motivation.

Step 4: Rebuild Psychological Capital

Psychological capital (PsyCap) - comprising hope, efficacy, resilience, and optimism - provides individuals and teams with necessary psychological resources for maintaining positivity in the face of challenges. Research has shown that PsyCap is positively associated with job satisfaction, organizational commitment, and performance while negatively associated with stress and turnover intentions (Luthans et al., 2007; Avey et al., 2011). Cultivating PsyCap can involve practices such as setting achievable goals to foster hope, providing training and support to enhance efficacy, promoting a culture of learning and growth to build resilience, and encouraging a positive outlook through regular recognition and celebration of successes.

Leaders can cultivate PsyCap through targeted training programs, coaching, and creating an environment that nurtures these qualities—for instance; they can build hope by involving employees in goal-setting and helping them map out pathways to achieve those goals, foster self-efficacy by providing stretch assignments with appropriate support, develop resilience through reframing setbacks and celebrating learning from failures, and reinforce optimism by highlighting progress and expressing confidence in people's abilities.

> Cultivating psychological capital equips individuals and teams with the mental resources needed to maintain positivity in the face of challenges.

Heather shared how they build psychological capital through regular practices: "We have these leadership huddles with people from all over the organization, and it starts with people submitting what they are grateful for or how they want to celebrate somebody else." This simple ritual leverages positive emotions and strengthens social bonds.

It is important to note that rebuilding psychological capital is not about forcing positivity or denying real challenges. Instead, it is about equipping people with the mental and emotional resources to respond to difficulties more constructively. As Erica put it, "In a negative work culture, people don't collaborate or take risks. They might avoid innovation because they fear getting in trouble for making mistakes. There's a lack of trust that prevents them from stepping out of their comfort zones." Building psychological capital creates safety for people to take risks, be vulnerable, and persevere through obstacles.

Step 5: Address Negativity Constructively

While cultivating positivity is crucial, it is equally important to have processes in place for addressing negativity when it does arise. Left unchecked, negativity can quickly spread and undermine transformation efforts. As Mel noted, "It can go viral if there is not a way to help see an alternative opinion." Addressing negativity constructively starts with creating psychological safety for people to voice concerns openly, actively soliciting feedback, and responding non-defensively. It also involves teaching and modeling healthy conflict-resolution skills. Many organizations I have worked with have implemented formal training programs in crucial conversations or nonviolent communication to give employees tools for addressing issues productively.

Leaders must be willing to engage directly with negative sources rather than avoid them. Thus, requiring difficult conversations and tough decisions. Peter insights shared, "If you don't address people's concerns, they'll stop coming to you with them. The problems won't go away - they'll just fester and grow without your knowledge. People will become resentful and feel helpless, while you'll be left in the dark, unaware of the issues building up."

At the same time, it is essential to maintain appropriate boundaries and not get pulled into negativity spirals. Leaders should focus on understanding root causes and collaborative problem-solving rather than commiserating or placing blame. Sometimes, persistent sources of negativity may need to be removed from the organization if they are unwilling to change and undermine the more significant cultural shift.

Step 6: Leverage Positivity and Celebrate Success

Sustaining cultural transformation requires ongoing leveraging of positive norms and behaviors. This involves consistently recognizing and rewarding actions that align with the desired culture. As Darin emphasized, "Leading by modeling is critical. Without it, other efforts may be futile. But even with a good example, you must reinforce it verbally and consistently."

Celebration is a powerful tool for leveraging positivity. This can take many forms, from public recognition in team meetings to formal award programs to impromptu expressions of gratitude. The key is making the celebration a regular, integral part of organizational life rather than an occasional afterthought. One tech company I worked with implemented a digital "kudos" system where employees could give each other points for helpful actions, redeemable for small rewards. Thus, it dramatically increased peer-to-peer recognition and reinforced a culture of appreciation.

Celebrating progress and learning, not just outcomes, is essential. It helps maintain momentum and resilience during long-term change efforts. Leaders should look for opportunities to highlight small wins and incremental improvements. For instance, a manufacturing plant I consulted with started tracking and celebrating "near misses"—potential safety incidents that were caught, prevented, and reinforced a proactive safety culture much more effectively than only focusing on actual incidents.

Navigating Challenges and Resistance to Change

Implementing this SPIRAL 6-step framework is not a linear process. Leaders should expect various challenges and sources of resistance along the way. Common obstacles include:

> 1. Entrenched negative mindsets: People habituated to negativity may initially resist efforts to shift the culture. They may see positive

initiatives as naive or insincere.

2. Lack of trust: Employees may be skeptical of new initiatives if there is a history of failed change efforts or breached promises.

3. Middle management bottleneck: Cultural change often energizes frontline employees and senior leaders, but middle managers need help translating it into day-to-day practices.

4. External pressures: Market challenges, regulatory constraints, or other external factors can create stress that makes it difficult to maintain positivity.

5. Impatience for results: Cultural change takes time, and some stakeholders may get frustrated if they do not see immediate improvements.

6. Conflicting subcultures: Different departments or locations may have developed distinct subcultures that are challenging to align.

> Cultural transformation is not a destination but an ongoing journey of spiraling up.

Navigating these challenges requires persistence, adaptability, and a systems-thinking approach. Leaders need to anticipate and plan for resistance while remaining open to feedback that may highlight legitimate concerns or blind spots in the change approach. Building a coalition of change champions at all levels of the organization is crucial for maintaining momentum. It is also important to set expectations correctly and communicate that cultural transformation is an ongoing journey rather than a destination. Small, consistent steps often prove more sustainable than grand, sweeping changes. As Darin advised, "It will take time for real change to happen. Models like SPIRAL are only helpful if we use them. Positivity needs to be a part of our culture. Our leaders need to commit to this process. I must constantly reinforce it, modeling these steps in my leadership."

Measuring Progress and Impact on Organizational Culture

Measuring the impact of cultural transformation efforts can be challenging, given the intangible nature of many cultural elements. However, it is crucial to establish clear metrics and regularly assess progress to maintain accountability and guide ongoing efforts. A holistic measurement approach should include both quantitative and qualitative indicators.

Quantitative metrics might include:

* Employee engagement scores
* Turnover rates
* Absenteeism
* Productivity measures
* Customer satisfaction ratings
* Financial performance indicators

Qualitative indicators could involve:

* Systematic analysis of internal communications
* Observational data on meeting dynamics and decision-making processes
* Employee focus groups and interviews
* Customer and partner feedback
* Leadership behavior assessments

Establishing a baseline at the outset of transformation efforts and tracking changes over time is essential. Leaders should also be open to emergent indicators that may arise during the change process. Regular pulse surveys can provide ongoing feedback on how employees are experiencing the cultural shift.

One simple way to begin identifying your metric is taking the Positivity Leadership Index. It can be utilized as a pre-post assessment to establish a baseline of your leadership competency and organization culture.

Scan to Take the PLX

Like the PLX, one healthcare organization I worked with developed a custom "positivity index" that combined quantitative metrics like employee net promoter score and qualitative assessments of language use in team meetings. This provided a holistic view of cultural health that guided leadership interventions. The most powerful measure of cultural transformation is sustained behavior change. Are people consistently demonstrating the desired mindsets and behaviors, even under stress or when leaders are absent? This requires ongoing observation and feedback loops to reinforce positive changes.

Surviving vs. Thriving Leaders! You do not have to go it alone!

In the early days of my coaching career, I stumbled upon a profound truth that would shape my approach to leadership development: No leader should go it alone. This realization crystallized during my first five years as a coach when I hosted a monthly CEO forum.

Every month, about a dozen executive leaders from diverse industries gather in a comfortable, safe setting. These individuals bear the weight of major decisions, the pressure of stakeholder expectations, and the loneliness that often accompanies positions of power in their daily lives. Yet, in this room, they find something invaluable: peers who understand their challenges, who can offer fresh perspectives, and genuinely care about each other's success.

I remember vividly the first few meetings. There was palpable tension in the air, a hesitancy to open fully. These were competitors in some cases and strangers in others. However, as the months went by, something remarkable began to unfold.

One CEO, Conor, came to the meeting visibly distressed. His company was facing a major crisis, and he felt paralyzed by the magnitude of the decision before him. As he shared his dilemma, the room fell silent. Then, one by one, his peers began to offer insights, share similar experiences, and ask probing questions that helped Conor see his situation from new angles. By the end of that session, Conor's demeanor had completely changed. The burden had not disappeared, but he now had a clear action plan and, more importantly, the confidence from knowing he was not alone in his struggle.

Similar scenes played out countless times over the years. Leaders who entered the room burdened and uncertain left with renewed energy, clear direction, and a support network they could lean on. The power of this peer group was undeniable. It provided a safe space for shared learning, where successes and failures could be dissected without judgment. It fostered accountability, as leaders committed to each other and reported on their progress. It encouraged transparency and vulnerability, allowing these strong individuals to admit their fears and doubts and, in doing so, find strength. What amazed me most was how this translated into their leadership. The confidence they gained from the peer group emboldened them to face difficulties head-on in their organizations. They became more open with their teams, fostering cultures of trust and collaboration.

I watched in awe as leaders transformed before my eyes. Their perspectives broadened, their confidence grew, and they developed a knack for turning the group's collective wisdom into clear, actionable steps. However, the impact did not stop with them. Like ripples in a pond, the effects spread throughout their organizations, influencing company culture, decision-making processes, and business outcomes. One

> Successful leaders recognize they shouldn't navigate the challenges of organizational transformation alone.

leader, inspired by the forum's approach, instituted a similar peer group within his company, bringing together department heads who had previously worked in silos. The result was a more cohesive, innovative organization that could respond more nimbly to market changes. These experiences underscored a crucial lesson: leadership does not have to be a solitary journey. It should not be. The most effective leaders recognize the value of community, seek out diverse perspectives, and are not afraid to say, "I do not have all the answers, but together, we can figure this out."

Remember that somewhere out there, in boardrooms, coffee shops, and online forums, leaders are coming together, sharing their challenges, and finding strength in each other. In doing so, they're not just becoming better leaders themselves—they're creating better, more human-centered organizations that are equipped to thrive in our complex, ever-changing world. After a decade of consulting and coaching, I have observed a clear distinction between leaders who merely survive and those who truly thrive in their roles. The differentiating factors consistently revolve around authentic leadership, a growth mindset, psychological capital, and the courage to address negativity head-on. Moreover, these successful leaders always lean into their support teams.

Authentic leadership forms the foundation of thriving leadership. A study published in the Journal of Business Ethics found that authentic leadership positively relates to employee job satisfaction, organizational commitment, and work engagement (Avolio et al., 2004). Leaders who demonstrate transparency, balanced information processing, self-awareness, and high ethical standards create an environment of trust and psychological safety. This, in turn, fosters innovation and employee well-being. Leaders with a growth mindset view challenges as opportunities for learning and development rather than insurmountable obstacles. Research published in the Harvard Business Review indicates that organizations with a growth mindset culture are 34% more likely to feel a keen sense of ownership and commitment to the company (Dweck, 2014). Psychological capital, comprising hope, efficacy, resilience, and optimism (HERO), is a powerful resource for leaders navigating complex and challenging environments. A meta-analysis published in the Journal of Management found that psychological capital positively relates to desirable employee attitudes, behaviors, and performance (Avey et al., 2011). Leaders who cultivate these qualities in themselves and their teams are better equipped to overcome adversity and maintain a positive organizational culture.

The courage to address negativity head-on is a distinguishing trait of thriving leaders. Rather than avoiding or suppressing negative emotions and experiences, these leaders create systems and processes to address and learn from them constructively. The Harvard Business Review reports that leaders who effectively manage conflict and address negativity can increase team performance by up to 40% (Gallo, 2017). Most importantly, successful leaders recognize they cannot and should not attempt to lead in isolation. They actively seek out mentorship, coaching, and peer support. The impact of these support systems is significant. A study by the International Coach Federation found that 80% of people who receive coaching support reported an increased self-confidence, and over 70% benefit from improved work performance, relationships, and more effective communication skills (ICF et al. Study, 2009). Furthermore, research published in the Leadership Quarterly suggests that leaders participating in peer advisory groups experience enhanced strategic decision-making capabilities and improved leadership effectiveness (Yip & Wilson, 2010). These peer groups provide a safe space for leaders to share challenges, gain diverse perspectives, and learn from others' experiences.

> Organizations that foster a growth mindset culture are 34% more likely to feel a strong sense of ownership and commitment to the company.

The commitment to leveraging these support systems is critical to overcoming negativity and driving positive change. A Center for Creative Leadership survey found that 88% of leaders believe leadership development is critical to their business success, yet only 31% believe their organization has the necessary leadership capacity (Petrie, 2014). This gap underscores the importance of investing in leadership development and support systems.

Successful leaders recognize overcoming negativity and fostering a positive organizational culture requires a systemic approach. The "Spiral Up" framework provides a strategic change system, allowing leaders to address negativity and build positive momentum systematically. This approach aligns with research on positive organizational scholarship, which suggests that focusing on positive deviance and strengths can lead to extraordinary performance (Cameron & Spreitzer, 2012).

Moreover, thriving leaders surround themselves with a dedicated support network of stakeholders committed to their success and positive progress. This network often includes board members, executive teams, external advisors, and family members. An Academy of Management Journal study found that CEOs with diverse and supportive social networks are likely to lead their organizations to higher performance (McDonald & Westphal, 2003).

In my consulting experience, I have seen firsthand how leaders who embrace these principles transform their organizations. One CEO of a mid-sized technology company was struggling with a toxic culture and high turnover. By committing to authentic leadership, rebuilding psychological capital in her team, and actively participating in a peer advisory group, she was able to turn the company around. Within two years, employee engagement scores increased by 40%, and the company's revenue grew by 25%. Another leader in the healthcare sector faced significant regulatory challenges and employee burnout. By adopting a growth mindset, addressing negativity constructively, and working closely with an executive coach, he implemented innovative solutions that not only met regulatory requirements but also improved patient outcomes and employee satisfaction.

These examples illustrate that thriving as a leader in today's complex business environment requires more than technical skills or industry knowledge. It demands a commitment to personal growth, cultivating positive psychological resources, and the wisdom to seek support and diverse perspectives. Leaders who thrive in the face of adversity and negativity authentically embody positive leadership principles, maintain a growth orientation, rebuild psychological capital, and bravely confront negativity. Most importantly, they recognize the power of community and support in their leadership journey. By leveraging mentorship, coaching, and peer groups, and by implementing strategic change systems like the Spiral Up framework, these leaders not only overcome negativity but also create thriving, positive organizations that are well-equipped to face the challenges of the modern business landscape.

Conclusion

Leading cultural transformation from negativity to positivity is a complex, long-term endeavor. It requires a comprehensive approach that addresses all organizational levels' mindsets, behaviors, systems, and norms. The six-step framework presented here provides a roadmap, but leaders must adapt it to their specific context and remain flexible as the journey unfolds. Emerging leaders, entrepreneurs, and executives can create lasting positive change by strengthening authentic leadership, pinpointing negativity's impact, inspiring positive mindsets, rebuilding psychological capital, addressing issues constructively, and leveraging positivity. This not only improves organizational performance but also enhances employee well-being and fulfillment. Cultivating positive organizational cultures is more important than ever in a world facing unprecedented challenges. It allows companies to attract and retain top talent, innovate more effectively, and better weather turbulent times. Most importantly, it creates workplaces where people can thrive and do their best work in service of a larger purpose.

Recap: Leading the Transformation - A Holistic Approach

Transforming an organization's culture from negativity to positivity requires a comprehensive, sustained effort led from the top. This chapter outlines a SPIRAL 6-step framework for cultural transformation and provides guidance on implementation, overcoming challenges, and measuring progress.

Key Insights:

* **The Power of Authentic Leadership**: Authentic leadership is the cornerstone of cultural transformation. By consistently aligning words with actions, being transparent about challenges, and genuinely caring for employees' well-being, leaders create the psychological safety necessary for positive change. This foundation of trust enables employees to voice concerns constructively and take risks in service of organizational improvement.

* **Negativity's Ripple Effect**: Unchecked negativity can quickly become entrenched in workplace norms, attitudes, and behaviors. Recognizing and addressing negativity's impact is crucial, as it can spread virally and shape the expectations of new employees. Leaders must be proactive in identifying sources of negativity and understanding their root causes to effectively combat this destructive force.

* **The Mindset Shift**: Transforming organizational culture requires a fundamental shift from a scarcity mindset to an abundance mindset. This involves reframing how people think about work, relationships, and challenges. Leaders play a pivotal role in this shift by consistently using language that focuses on possibilities, learning opportunities, and strengths rather than limitations and problems.

* **Psychological Capital as a Resource**: Rebuilding psychological capital (PsyCap) - comprising hope, efficacy, resilience, and optimism - equips individuals and teams with the mental resources needed to maintain positivity in the face of challenges. By investing in practices that build PsyCap, organizations can create a more resilient workforce capable of navigating change and adversity with a positive outlook.

* **The Collective Power of Leadership Support**: Successful leaders recognize that they shouldn't navigate the challenges of organizational transformation alone. Leveraging support systems such as mentorship, coaching, and peer advisory groups not only enhances a leader's effectiveness but also provides fresh perspectives and shared learning experiences. This collective approach to leadership development can significantly accelerate positive cultural change.

Leadership Reflection Questions:

1. How do I currently embody authentic leadership in my daily interactions with my team? What areas can I improve?

2. In what ways might I inadvertently be contributing to negativity in my organization? How can I address these behaviors?

3. How effectively am I rebuilding psychological capital (hope, efficacy, resilience, and optimism) in myself and my team?

4. What systems or processes in our organization might unintentionally reinforce negativity? How can we modify them to support a more positive culture?

5. How am I currently leveraging support systems (mentors, coaches, peer groups) in my leadership journey? What additional support might be beneficial?

Team-Building Activity: Working an Issue

Objective: To simulate a peer learning experience where leaders can present challenges, receive thoughtful questions, and develop action steps with group support.

Duration: Approximately 90-120 minutes (3 rounds of 30-40 minutes each)

Materials Needed:
- Timer
- Notepads and pens for each participant
- Optional: Whiteboard or flip chart for capturing insights

Participants:
- 6-12 team members
- 1 dedicated facilitator (if possible)

Instructions:

1. Setup (5 minutes):
    - Arrange seating in a circle to promote open discussion.
    - The facilitator explains the process and emphasizes the importance of confidentiality and psychological safety.

2. Round Structure (30-40 minutes per round): a. Issue Presentation (5 minutes):
    - One person presents a current leadership challenge or issue.
    - They may use a written summary or a brief PowerPoint for clarity.

3. Questioning Period (15-20 minutes):

- Group members ask meaningful, open-ended questions to help the presenter gain new perspectives.

- Avoid giving advice or proposing solutions.

- The facilitator ensures questions remain constructive and on-topic.

4. Reflection and Action Planning (10-15 minutes):

    - The presenter reflects on the discussion and shares:
        - Key insights gained
        - Concrete action steps they plan to take
        - Support they need from the group over the next month

5. Rotation:

    - Take a 5-minute break between rounds to reset.
    - Move to the next presenter and repeat the process.

6. Closing Reflection (10 minutes):

    - After all rounds, the facilitator leads a brief closing discussion.
    - Each participant shares one insight they gained about their own leadership from the exercise.

Facilitator Notes:
- Ensure strict timekeeping to allow equal time for each presenter.

- Encourage depth over breadth in questioning.

- Remind participants to focus on asking questions rather than providing solutions.

- Guide the group to commit to specific support actions for each presenter.

Follow-up:
- Schedule a check-in one month later for presenters to update the group on their progress and any additional support needed.

This "Working an Issue" activity provides a structured yet flexible format for peer learning and support. It aligns with the chapter's insights on the importance of leadership support systems and the value of diverse perspectives in addressing organizational challenges. By focusing on asking meaningful questions rather than providing quick fixes, it encourages deeper reflection and more sustainable solutions to complex leadership issues. Asking better questions often leads to better outcomes. Thus, the peer group grows together in courage to ask the challenge questions while providing the needed support for the one presenting the issue. It's a training group to develop leaders and manager's ability to do the same with their direct reports and teams. Aligning to the metaphor of Spiraling Up, for the one presenting, the exercise provides the gift of perspective working together, seeing the opportunity or challenge from multiple perspectives, resulting in clarity of the "real issue" to avoid preoccupation with resourcing what's secondary.

Chapter 10
Spiraling Up - Sustaining a Positive Workplace Culture

As we conclude *Spiraling Up*, we have been on a journey through the landscape of positive workplace culture; it is fitting to reflect on the rich tapestry of insights and experiences that have shaped this exploration. This final chapter is not merely a culmination of ideas but a testament to the power of perseverance, authenticity, and continuous growth in the face of organizational challenges. Drawing from the wisdom of 12 executive interviews, the rigorous analysis of over 150 peer-reviewed articles in my dissertation literature review, and the countless coaching conversations that have been the bedrock of my work in changing and sustaining positive cultures, a profound truth emerges: the path to a thriving workplace is neither linear nor easily charted, but it is infinitely rewarding.

Throughout this journey, I have had the privilege of being a facilitator and thought partner to many authentic, courageous leaders. There is a lot of grit, grind, and get up again, then again in their leadership. Stories of triumph, struggle, small victories, and daunting setbacks have illuminated the real-world application of positive psychology principles in the workplace. No leader is perfect, yet the most impactful ones share a common trait: the courage to engage in honest conversations and a steadfast commitment to positive change over the long haul. These leaders press forward amid challenges, recognizing that cultural transformation is not a destination but an ongoing process of spiraling up.

Transforming an organization's culture from negativity to positivity is not a linear path with a definitive endpoint. Instead, it is an ongoing process of spiraling up - continuously reinforcing and elevating positive mindsets, behaviors, and practices throughout the organization. This chapter explores how to sustain and deepen cultural transformation efforts over the long term, moving beyond initial interventions to embed positivity into the organization's DNA. Drawing on insights from the research conducted for this dissertation, executive interviews, and my consulting experiences, we will examine strategies for anchoring positivity in organizational values, empowering employees as champions of cultural change, and fostering a mindset of continuous learning and improvement. This journey towards a positive workplace culture is possible and promising, offering a beacon of hope for organizations seeking to thrive in a rapidly changing world.

Embedding Positivity into Organizational Values, Norms, and Practices

> Sustaining a positive workplace culture requires embedding positivity into organizational values, norms, and daily practices.

Positivity must be woven into how the company operates daily to become genuinely ingrained in an organization's culture. DNA goes beyond surface-level initiatives or temporary programs to fundamentally reshape core values, behavioral norms, and operational practices. As Darin emphasized, "Positivity needs to be a part of our culture. I need to reinforce it, modeling these steps in my leadership constantly." This sentiment underscores the need for a holistic, sustained approach to cultural transformation, with leaders at the forefront, driving the change and setting the tone for a positive workplace culture.

A crucial first step is explicitly incorporating positivity into the organization's stated values and mission. This signals to all stakeholders that cultivating a positive workplace is a strategic priority, not just a nice-to-have. For instance, one technology company I worked with revised its core values to include "Cultivate Joy" alongside more traditional values like innovation and customer focus. This simple addition sparked meaningful conversations about what brings people joy at work and how to amplify those elements. It is essential that these values are not just platitudes on a wall but actively lived and reinforced throughout the organization. Leaders should regularly reference these values in decision-making, performance evaluations, and strategic planning efforts.

Embedding Positivity also requires reshaping behavioral norms - the unwritten rules that govern how people interact and work together. Reshaping involves both encouraging positive behaviors and actively discouraging negative ones. For example, one healthcare organization implemented a "no triangulation" policy, where employees were expected to address conflicts directly with the person involved rather than complaining to others. Straight talk dramatically reduced gossip and backstabbing, creating a more open and constructive communication culture. Another company instituted a practice of starting all meetings by sharing a recent success or expressing gratitude, setting a positive tone for discussions. Over time, these practices become habitual, shaping how people naturally behave, even without explicit prompting.

Operational practices and systems are crucial in sustaining a positive culture. Front-loading employee expectations include hiring and onboarding processes, performance management systems, and communication channels. Each of these touchpoints offers an opportunity to reinforce positive values and behaviors. For instance, one retail company revised its hiring criteria to explicitly assess candidates' positivity and resilience alongside technical skills. Thus, improving cultural fitness leads to better long-term performance and retention. Similarly, a manufacturing firm redesigned its performance review process to focus on strengths and growth opportunities rather than deficits, aligning with a more positive, developmental approach.

Technology plays a pivotal role in embedding positivity into daily operations. It provides efficient and effective communication and feedback, enhancing the reader's understanding of its impact on sustaining a positive culture. Many organizations leverage digital platforms to facilitate peer recognition, share success stories, and provide real-time feedback. One global consulting firm I worked with implemented a mobile app where employees could give each other "micro-bonuses" for helpful actions, creating constant positive reinforcement. Another company used an AI-powered chatbot to regularly check in with employees on their mood and engagement, providing an early warning system for potential issues and celebrating positive trends.

The physical environment also plays a vital role in sustaining a positive culture. The design of workspaces can either facilitate or hinder positive interactions and behaviors. One creative agency redesigned its office to include more collaborative spaces and quiet reflection areas, supporting energizing teamwork and individual recharging. They also incorporated visual reminders of the company's positive mission and employee achievements throughout the space, even in remote or hybrid work environments, virtual space design matters. For instance, some companies are creating digital "water coolers" or informal chat channels to replicate the spontaneous, positive interactions in physical offices.

Ultimately, embedding positivity into organizational DNA requires constant attention and reinforcement. It requires more than a few initiatives and more than expecting the culture to maintain itself. Leaders must continually look for opportunities to align all aspects of the organization—from high-level strategy to day-to-day operations—with the desired positive culture. This ongoing effort creates a virtuous cycle, where positive behaviors beget more positive behaviors, truly spiraling up over time.

Empowering Employees to Be Champions of Positivity

While leadership commitment is crucial for cultural transformation, lasting change requires engagement and ownership from employees at all levels of the organization. Empowering employees to become active champions of positivity creates a multiplier effect, accelerating and deepening cultural shifts. As Melanie noted in our interviews, "I believe I contributed to changing our organizational culture by demonstrating genuine respect for my colleagues. This meant valuing their opinions and ideas, and actively showing that I welcomed their input. By fostering an environment where team collaboration was appreciated and encouraged, I helped shift our workplace towards a more inclusive and participative culture." This collaborative approach generates more ideas for fostering positivity and increases buy-in and sustainability of change efforts, making every employee feel valued and integral to the process.

A key strategy for empowering employees is to create formal roles and structures dedicated to cultural positivity. Many organizations are establishing "culture committees" or "positivity ambassadors" drawn from diverse company areas. These groups generate ideas, plan initiatives, and advocate for the desired culture. For instance, one financial services firm I consulted with created a "Joy Champions" network in each department. These volunteers received special training in positive psychology principles and were given time and resources to implement small-scale experiments to boost workplace positivity. This distributed approach allowed for tailored interventions that resonated with different subcultures within the organization.

> Empowering employees to become active champions of positivity creates a multiplier effect, accelerating and deepening cultural shifts.

Training and skill development are also crucial for empowering employees to champion positivity, and beyond explaining the importance of a positive culture, equipping people with practical tools and techniques is essential. Many companies invest in programs focused on emotional intelligence, resilience, strengths-based development, and positive communication. For example, one technology company rolled out a company-wide training on the PERMA model of well-being (Positive emotions, Engagement, Relationships, Meaning, and Accomplishment), giving employees a shared language and framework for discussing and cultivating positivity. Another organization implemented regular "positivity workouts" - short, focused sessions where teams practiced specific techniques like reframing negative situations or expressing appreciation.

Empowerment also means giving employees the autonomy and resources to foster positivity, creating innovation funds for culture-related projects, allowing teams to experiment with new working methods, or encouraging grassroots efforts to spread positivity. One manufacturing plant I worked with established a "Culture Improvement Kaizen" process, where any employee could propose and lead a small project to enhance workplace positivity, mirroring their continuous improvement approach to operations. Generating many creative ideas increased employees' sense of ownership over the culture.

Recognition and celebration play a crucial role in empowering positivity champions. It is essential to visibly acknowledge and reward efforts to enhance the workplace culture, reinforcing that these contributions are valued alongside more traditional performance metrics. Many organizations are incorporating cultural impact into their formal recognition programs. For instance, one healthcare system created a monthly "Culture Builder" award, celebrating employees who went above and beyond in fostering a positive environment. These stories were widely shared, inspiring others to take similar actions.

Empowering employees also involves creating platforms for open dialogue about culture and well-being. These forums include regular town halls, anonymous feedback channels, or cross-functional discussion groups. The key is creating safe spaces where people feel comfortable sharing positive experiences and constructive concerns. One tech company I advised implemented quarterly "Culture Cafes"—informal gatherings where employees could discuss cultural topics with senior leaders in a relaxed setting. Thus, valuable insights surfaced, and trust and transparency increased across hierarchical levels.

It is important to note that empowerment does not mean abdicating leadership responsibility for cultural transformation. Instead, it is about creating the conditions for widespread engagement and initiative-taking around positivity. Leaders still play a crucial role in setting the overall direction, modeling desired behaviors, and removing obstacles to positive change. The goal is to create a symbiotic relationship where top-down guidance and bottom-up energy reinforce each other, accelerating the upward spiral of positivity.

Continuous Learning and Improvement for Leaders and Teams

A positive workplace culture requires ongoing learning, adaptation, and growth commitment. The work landscape constantly evolves, bringing new challenges and opportunities that impact organizational culture. Leaders and teams must, therefore, cultivate a mindset of continuous improvement, regularly reflecting on what is working and what is not and how to evolve their approach to fostering positivity. As Heather shared in our interviews, "Our leaders need to commit to this process. I must constantly reinforce it, modeling these steps in my leadership." This highlights the importance of persistent effort and ongoing learning in cultural transformation.

A foundational element of continuous improvement is establishing robust feedback loops. Leaders regularly gather data on the state of the culture from multiple sources and use those insights to inform ongoing efforts. Many organizations are moving beyond annual engagement surveys to more frequent pulse checks and real-time feedback mechanisms. For instance, one retail company I worked with implemented a daily one-question poll asking employees to rate their mood and optionally provide comments. This data was aggregated into a "cultural weather report" that leaders could use to quickly identify and address emerging issues. Another firm used sentiment analysis on internal communication platforms to track trends in language use and emotional tone, providing an ongoing measure of cultural health.

Continuous learning also requires creating intentional spaces for reflection and dialogue about cultural efforts. Regular retrospectives where teams discuss what is working well and what could be improved regarding workplace positivity. Many organizations are incorporating cultural topics into existing meeting rhythms, such as dedicating time to quarterly business reviews to discuss cultural metrics alongside financial ones. Leadership teams should also continuously reflect on their role in shaping culture.

> Continuous learning and improvement are essential for adapting positivity practices to evolving organizational needs.

One executive team I advised on instituted a monthly "culture check" where they candidly discussed how their behaviors and decisions impacted the broader organizational culture.

Staying abreast of emerging research and best practices in positive organizational scholarship is another crucial aspect of continuous improvement. The field of positive psychology and its applications to the workplace are rapidly evolving, offering new insights and tools for fostering individual and collective well-being. Many companies are partnering with academic institutions or bringing in external experts to stay current on the latest developments. For example, one technology firm established a "Positive Work Lab" in collaboration with a local university, conducting applied research on innovative approaches to enhancing workplace positivity. The Lab informed their practices and contributed to the broader body of knowledge in the field.

Cross-pollination of ideas across industries and sectors can also spark valuable insights for cultural improvement. Many organizations create opportunities for leaders and teams to learn from diverse contexts. It could involve executive exchanges, cross-industry learning cohorts, or simply encouraging employees to seek inspiration from unexpected sources. One healthcare system I worked with sent teams to visit companies in hospitality and retail to gain fresh perspectives on creating cheerful customer (and employee) experiences. These external viewpoints often highlight blind spots or inspire creative approaches that would not have emerged within the industry bubble.

Experimentation and piloting are crucial tools for continuous improvement in cultural transformation efforts. Many organizations are adopting a more iterative, test-and-learn approach rather than trying to implement sweeping changes simultaneously. Running small-scale experiments with new practices or interventions, carefully measuring the impact, and then refining or scaling based on the results. For instance, one manufacturing company piloted a "positivity pause" - a brief daily team check-in focused on sharing good news and expressing gratitude - in a single department before rolling it out more broadly. The pause allowed them to work out kinks and build evidence of impact, increasing buy-in for the more comprehensive implementation.

Technology can be a powerful enabler of continuous learning and improvement in cultural efforts. Many organizations are leveraging digital platforms to facilitate knowledge sharing, collaboration, and real-time adaptation of positivity practices. For example, one global consulting firm created an internal "Culture Wiki" where employees could share successful positivity interventions, lessons learned, and resources. This living repository allowed for rapid dissemination of best practices across the organization. Another company used machine learning algorithms to analyze patterns in their cultural data, identifying leading indicators of cultural health and suggesting personalized interventions for different teams.

It is important to note that continuous improvement in cultural transformation is not just about adding new initiatives or tweaking existing ones. It also involves regularly reassessing and potentially sunsetting practices that no longer serve the desired culture. This requires a willingness to let go of "sacred cows" and adapt to changing needs. Upon closer examination, one retail organization I advised had a long-standing employee recognition program reinforcing siloed behavior counter to their desired collaborative culture. By acknowledging this misalignment and redesigning the program, they could better align recognition with their evolving cultural aspirations.

> Technology can be a powerful enabler of continuous learning and improvement in cultural efforts.

Leadership development plays a crucial role in supporting the continuous improvement of organizational culture. As the drivers and role models of cultural change, leaders must constantly evolve their capabilities to foster positivity. Many organizations are incorporating positive leadership principles into their core leadership development curricula. This includes strengths-based management, cultivating psychological safety, and leading with compassion. Some companies also provide specialized training and coaching for leaders specifically focused on cultural stewardship. For instance, one technology firm implemented a "Culture Catalyst" program for high-potential leaders, equipping them with advanced skills in change management, positive psychology, and systems thinking applied to cultural transformation.

Conclusion: The Ongoing Journey of Spiraling Up

Sustaining a positive workplace culture is not a destination but an ongoing journey of spiraling up. It requires constant attention, adaptation, and renewal to embed positivity deeply into organizational DNA, empower employees as culture champions, and foster continuous learning and improvement. This journey is rarely smooth or linear - there will inevitably be setbacks, resistance, and unexpected challenges along the way. However, organizations can create an upward spiral of cultural health and performance by maintaining a long-term commitment to positivity and leveraging the strategies outlined in this chapter.

The benefits of this sustained effort are profound. Research has consistently shown that positive workplace cultures lead to higher employee engagement, creativity, and productivity (Cameron et al., 2003; Fredrickson, 2003). They also contribute to better customer experiences, more robust financial performance, and greater organizational resilience in facing challenges (Luthans et al., 2007; Avey et al., 2011). Most importantly, positive cultures create environments where people can thrive, find meaning in their work, and contribute their best selves.

> The journey of spiraling up creates workplaces where people can thrive, find meaning in their work, and contribute their best selves.

As we navigate an increasingly complex and uncertain business landscape, cultivating and sustaining positive organizational cultures will become an increasingly critical competitive advantage. The organizations that master this art of spiraling up—continuously reinforcing and elevating positivity throughout their systems—will be positioned to attract top talent, innovate rapidly, and create lasting value for all stakeholders.

Cultural transformation is not easy, but it is gratifying. It requires courage, persistence, and a genuine belief in the potential for positive change. As leaders and organizations embrace this journey, they can transform their workplaces and contribute to a broader shift towards a world where work is a source of joy, growth, and meaningful contribution for all.

Recap: Sustaining A Positive Workplace Culture

The process of "spiraling up" - continuously reinforcing and elevating positive mindsets, behaviors, and practices throughout an organization. It emphasizes that transforming workplace culture is not a linear path but an ongoing journey that requires embedding positivity into organizational values, empowering employees, and fostering continuous learning and improvement.

5 Key Insights:

* **Leadership Commitment**: "Positivity needs to be a part of our culture. Leading by example is critical. Our leaders need to commit to this process. I must constantly reinforce it, modeling these steps in my leadership." This quote underscores the crucial role of leadership in driving and sustaining cultural change.

* **Embedding Positivity in Organizational DNA**: "For positivity to become genuinely ingrained in an organization's culture, it must be woven into how the company operates daily. This goes beyond surface-level initiatives or temporary programs to fundamentally reshape core values, behavioral norms, and operational practices." This insight highlights the need for a comprehensive approach to cultural transformation.

* **Employee Empowerment**: "Empowering employees to become active champions of positivity creates a multiplier effect, accelerating and deepening cultural shifts." This quote emphasizes the importance of engaging all levels of the organization in the cultural transformation process.

* **Continuous Learning and Improvement**: "Leaders and teams must, therefore, cultivate a mindset of continuous improvement, regularly reflecting on what is working and what is not and how to evolve their approach to fostering positivity." This insight stresses the need for ongoing adaptation and growth in maintaining a positive culture.

* **Technology as an Enabler**: "Technology plays a pivotal role in embedding positivity into daily operations. It provides efficient and effective communication and feedback, enhancing the reader's understanding of its impact on sustaining a positive culture." This quote highlights the role of Technology in facilitating and sustaining positive workplace cultures.

> **5 Leadership Reflection Questions:**
>
> 1. How am I personally modeling and reinforcing positive behaviors in my daily interactions with my team?
>
> 2. What structures or processes can we implement to empower employees to take the initiative to foster positivity?
>
> 3. How can we improve our feedback mechanisms to gather more real-time insights into our organizational culture?
>
> 4. How can we better integrate cultural metrics and discussions into our business reviews and strategic planning?
>
> 5. How can we create more opportunities to cross-pollinate ideas and learn from diverse contexts to enhance our approach to positive culture?

Team Building Activity: Positivity Hackathon

Objective: To engage teams in collaboratively generating and implementing ideas to enhance workplace positivity.

Duration: 2-4 hours

Materials: Flipcharts, markers, sticky notes, timer

Steps:

1. Introduction (10 minutes): Explain the concept of a "Positivity Hackathon" - a concentrated effort to generate and prototype ideas for enhancing workplace positivity.

2. Idea Generation (30 minutes): Divide participants into small groups. Each group brainstorms ideas for fostering positivity in the workplace, writing each on a sticky note.

3. Idea Clustering (15 minutes): Groups categorize their ideas into themes (e.g., recognition, communication, work environment).

4. Concept Development (45 minutes): Each group selects one idea to develop further, creating a brief proposal including the concept, potential impact, and implementation plan.

5. Pitch Preparation (20 minutes): Groups prepare a 3-minute pitch for their idea.

6. Pitching Session (30 minutes): Each group presents their idea to the larger team.

7. Voting and Selection (15 minutes): All participants vote on the ideas they find most impactful and feasible.

8. Action Planning (30 minutes): For the top-voted ideas, create action plans for piloting or implementing them in the workplace.

9. Reflection (15 minutes): Discuss lessons learned from the process

and how to maintain momentum in fostering positivity.

Follow-up: Schedule check-ins to track progress on implemented ideas and share successes with the broader organization.

This activity embodies the chapter's emphasis on employee empowerment, continuous improvement, and creating spaces for dialogue about cultural enhancement.

Chapter 11

Final Thought - Be the Catalyst for Change You Hope to See

As we conclude this exploration of transforming workplace negativity into positivity, it's clear that the journey of "Spiraling Up" is both challenging and profoundly rewarding. The research conducted for this dissertation, insights from executive interviews, and my own experiences as a consultant all point to a fundamental truth: leaders play a pivotal role in shaping organizational culture and have the power to create environments where people and businesses can thrive. The six-step framework presented in this book - fostering authentic leadership, recognizing negativity's impact, reframing mindsets, and expectations, cultivating psychological capital, addressing negativity constructively, and reinforcing positivity - provides a roadmap for this transformation. However, implementing these steps requires more than just technical knowledge; it demands a deep commitment to personal growth, emotional intelligence, and a genuine belief in the potential for positive change.

One of the key takeaways from this work is the critical importance of authentic leadership in driving cultural transformation. As Carolyn said during our interview, "Trust forms the foundation of respect. Without respect, the entire relationship crumbles." Authentic leaders build trust through consistent alignment between words and actions, transparency about challenges and mistakes, and genuine care for employees' wellbeing. This provides the psychological safety necessary for employees to voice concerns constructively, take risks in service of positive change, and fully engage in their work. The research shows that when leaders model authenticity, vulnerability, and a growth mindset, it catalyzes a ripple effect throughout the organization, gradually shifting norms and behaviors in a more positive direction.

Another crucial insight is the power of reframing negativity and cultivating psychological capital. The negativity bias is deeply ingrained in human psychology, making it easy for workplace cultures to spiral downward if left unchecked. However, by consciously reframing challenges as opportunities for growth and fostering hope, efficacy, resilience, and optimism (the components of psychological capital), leaders can help their teams develop the mental and emotional resources to thrive even under challenging circumstances. As Mel simply stated, "It's all about the spiraling up of the dialogue versus the spiraling down." This shift in perspective doesn't deny real problems but equips people to approach them more constructively and creatively.

The research also underscores the importance of systemic thinking in cultural transformation efforts. Negativity often becomes entrenched through organizational systems, processes, and norms that inadvertently reinforce it. Leaders must examine how performance management, communication channels, decision-making processes, and other organizational elements may contribute to negativity and realign them to support a more positive culture. This systemic approach, combined with individual mindset and behavior change, creates a powerful synergy for transformation. In my consulting work, I've seen how even minor adjustments to organizational practices can impact cultural health when aligned with a broader positivity initiative.

A critical challenge for leaders embarking on this journey is patience and persistence. Cultural transformation is complex: it requires sustained effort over time to shift profoundly ingrained thinking and behavior patterns. One executive noted, "It will take time for real change to happen. The SPIRAL 6-step model is good only if we use it. Positivity needs to be a part of our culture. Leading by example is critical. This long-term perspective can be challenging in a business world often focused on quarterly results. Still, the research shows that investments in positive culture pay off in improved engagement, innovation, and performance over time. This reiteration should make leaders feel determined and focused on the journey ahead.

Spiraling Up highlights the importance of empowering employees at all levels to become champions of positivity. While leadership sets the tone, lasting cultural change requires broad-based engagement and ownership. Creating formal roles like "culture ambassadors," providing training in positive psychology principles, and giving employees autonomy to initiate positivity projects can have a multiplier effect, accelerating the upward spiral. Many organizations I've worked with have found that their most impactful cultural initiatives originated from frontline employees when given the space and support to contribute.

A critical insight that emerged from research and practical experiences is the need for continuous learning and adaptation in cultural transformation efforts. The journey of spiraling up is dynamic; it requires ongoing reflection, measurement, and refinement of approaches. Leaders must stay attuned to emerging research in positive organizational scholarship, experiment with new practices, and regularly gather feedback to understand what's working and needs adjustment. This commitment to continuous improvement ensures that cultural transformation efforts remain relevant and impactful as the organization evolves.

The call to action for leaders is clear: embrace your role as architects of organizational culture and commit to spiraling up. This means implementing the strategies outlined in this book and embarking on a personal journey of growth and self-reflection. Authentic leadership starts with deep self-awareness and a willingness to confront biases, fears, and limiting beliefs. This inner work is not only challenging but also holds the potential for profound personal growth and transformation, which is essential for leading cultural transformation effectively.

The potential impact of this work extends far beyond individual organizations. In a world facing unprecedented challenges - from climate change to social inequality to technological disruption - we desperately need workplaces that bring out the best in people and contribute positively to society. By creating environments where people can thrive, find meaning in their work, and fully express their talents, leaders not only improve business outcomes but also have the power to make a meaningful difference in people's lives and the broader community. This realization should instill a sense of responsibility and purpose in leaders.

The transformative power of authentic leadership in overcoming negativity and unlocking human potential cannot be overstated. When leaders commit to fostering positivity, they set a virtuous cycle that elevates the entire organization. Employees become more engaged, creative, and resilient. Teams collaborate more effectively and innovate more readily. The organization becomes more adaptive and better able to navigate challenges. Most importantly, work becomes a source of fulfillment and growth rather than stress and burnout.

In conclusion, the journey of spiraling from negativity to positivity is not easy, but it is immensely worthwhile. It requires courage, persistence, and a genuine belief in the potential for positive change. To the leaders reading this: you have within you the power to transform your workplace and, by extension, to contribute to a more positive, humane, and flourishing world. The framework and insights in this book offer a starting point, but the real work begins with your commitment to lead authentically and foster positivity daily. As you embark on or continue this journey, remember that each small positive action, reframed perspective, and moment of genuine connection with your team members contribute to the upward spiral. The challenges are real, but so is the potential for transformation. The choice to lead positively is yours – and the impact of that choice can be profound.

Chapter 12
Bonus Chapter - The Positivity Flywheel

*S*PIRALING *U*P IS FUNDAMENTALLY about movement and momentum. It encapsulates the dynamic process of cultural transformation within organizations, where positive changes build upon each other, creating an upward spiral of improvement. This journey isn't linear; it's a cyclical, continuous growth, and refinement process. Like any change management cycle, it has factors that can initiate, accelerate, slow, or even halt progress. Understanding these factors is crucial for leaders aiming to fuel the engine of positive culture change.

At the heart of this upward spiral is the 'Positivity Flywheel,' a powerful metaphor that not only helps us visualize but also inspires us to understand the mechanics of cultural transformation. Just as a mechanical flywheel stores and releases energy to maintain steady motion in machinery, an organizational Positivity Flywheel generates and sustains momentum for positive cultural change. This Flywheel doesn't spin independently - it requires intentional effort to start and maintain its rotation. However, once in motion, it can create a self-reinforcing positivity cycle that permeates the organization, inspiring us with its potential for transformative change. Mechanically, a flywheel is a heavy rotating disk storing rotational energy in mechanical systems. Its primary purpose is to resist changes in rotational speed, providing stability and continuous motion. When power is applied to a flywheel, it speeds up, storing kinetic energy. As external energy input decreases, the Flywheel releases its stored energy, maintaining consistent motion and smoothing out fluctuations in the system.

The Organizational Positivity Flywheel

In an organizational context, the Positivity Flywheel represents the accumulation and momentum of positive cultural elements. These elements can include trust, psychological safety, engagement, purpose, resilience, open communication, continuous learning, recognition, empathy, and innovation. Like its mechanical counterpart, the Positivity Flywheel requires initial energy input to start spinning but becomes increasingly self-sustaining as it gains momentum. The Positivity Flywheel affects the entire organization, influencing everything from individual employee experiences to team dynamics and overall organizational performance.

Framework of the Positivity Flywheel

The Positivity Flywheel comprises several interconnected characteristics that work together to create and maintain positive momentum:

>1. *Trust:* The foundation upon which all positive interactions are built.
>2. *Psychological Safety:* An environment where people feel safe to take interpersonal risks.
>3. *Engagement:* Active participation and investment in work and organizational goals.
>4. *Purpose:* A clear sense of meaning and impact in one's work.
>5. *Resilience:* The ability to bounce back from setbacks and challenges.
>6. *Open Communication:* Free flow of information and ideas throughout the organization.
>7. *Continuous Learning:* A culture of growth and development.
>8. *Recognition:* Acknowledgment and celebration of contributions and achievements.
>9. *Empathy:* Understanding and sharing the feelings of others.

10. *Innovation:* Encouragement of new ideas and creative problem-solving.

Starting the Flywheel

Initiating the Positivity Flywheel requires deliberate effort and energy from organizational leaders. Key actions that start the flywheel spinning include:

1. *Authentic Leadership:* Leader's model vulnerability, transparency, and alignment between words and actions.
2. *Creating Psychological Safety:* Establishing an environment where people feel safe to voice concerns and take risks.
3. *Articulating a Compelling Vision:* Communicating a positive future state that inspires and motivates.
4. *Investing in Employee Development:* Demonstrating commitment to people's growth and potential.
5. *Implementing Fair and Transparent Processes:* Building trust through equitable systems and decision-making.
6. *Encouraging Collaboration:* Fostering teamwork and breaking down silos.
7. *Celebrating Early Wins:* Recognizing and amplifying positive changes, no matter how small.

As these actions gain traction, they create positive experiences and outcomes that feedback into the system, gradually increasing Flywheel's momentum.

Maintaining the Flywheel's Momentum

Once the Positivity Flywheel is in motion, it becomes easier to maintain its spin. However, consistent effort is still required to keep it moving smoothly:

1. *Consistent Communication:* Regularly reinforcing the organization's vision and values.
2. *Ongoing Feedback and Recognition:* Continuously acknowledging and rewarding positive behaviors and outcomes.
3. *Leadership Development:* Cultivating positive leadership practices at all levels of the organization.
4. *Continuous Improvement:* Regularly assessing and refining organizational processes and practices.
5. *Community Building:* Fostering solid relationships and a sense of belonging among employees.
6. *Alignment of Systems and Culture:* Ensuring formal structures support and reinforce the desired positive culture.

Slowing or Stopping the Flywheel

Several factors can slow or stop the Positivity Flywheel:

1. *Inconsistent Leadership:* Leaders are not "walking the talk" or demonstrating behaviors contradicting stated values.
2. *Unaddressed Negativity:* Allowing toxic behaviors or attitudes to persist without intervention.
3. *Lack of Follow-through:* Failing to act on employee feedback or promised initiatives.
4. *External Pressures:* Economic downturns, market disruptions, or other external challenges that create stress and uncertainty.
5. *Change Fatigue:* Overwhelming employees with too many initiatives or changes simultaneously.
6. *Neglecting Core Values:* Prioritizing short-term gains over long-term cultural health.
7. *Breakdown in Communication:* Lack of transparency or failure to keep people informed during challenging times.

When these factors arise, they create friction in the system, slowing the Flywheel's rotation and potentially reversing progress if not addressed promptly.

The Positivity Flywheel in Action

Imagine a technology company that transforms its culture from cutthroat competition to collaborative innovation. The leadership team starts by articulating this new vision and demonstrating authentic commitment to change. They implement new cross-functional collaboration and idea-sharing processes, invest in training programs to build creativity and teamwork skills and revise performance metrics to reward cooperative behaviors. Initially, progress may be slow as employees adjust to the new expectations. However, as people begin to experience the benefits of the innovative approach—a more enjoyable work environment, increased innovation, and better work-life balance—they become more engaged and invested in maintaining the positive momentum. This, in turn, attracts like-minded talent to the organization, further accelerating the Flywheel's spin. Over time, the positive culture becomes self-reinforcing. New hires are quickly acculturated to the collaborative mindset, teams naturally work together to solve problems, and the company gains a reputation for innovation and employee satisfaction. The Positivity Flywheel is spinning rapidly, providing stability even when faced with market challenges or leadership changes.

Integrating the Framework and Flywheel

While the Positivity Flywheel provides a powerful metaphor for cultural transformation, it's essential to recognize that sustainable change requires a holistic, systematic approach. This is where the 6-step framework for leading transformation comes into play, providing a structured roadmap for leaders to follow. The 6-step framework supports the momentum of the Positivity Flywheel, offering specific strategies for each phase of the transformation journey. Let's explore how these steps integrate with the flywheel metaphor:

1. *Foster Authentic Leadership*

Authentic leadership is the prime mover of the Positivity Flywheel. It provides the initial energy input to overcome inertia and start spinning the Flywheel. Authentic leaders build trust through consistent alignment between words and actions, transparency about challenges and mistakes, and genuine care for employees' well-being.

For example, a CEO who openly admits to a strategic misstep and involves employees in developing a corrective plan demonstrates vulnerability and trust in their team. This authenticity creates psychological safety, encouraging others to take similar risks in service of organizational goals.

2. *Recognize Negativity's Impact*

Before the Positivity Flywheel can gain significant momentum, leaders must understand what's slowing or stopping it. This step thoroughly assesses how negativity manifests in the organization and its impact on individuals, teams, and overall performance.

Leaders should gather both quantitative and qualitative data to build a comprehensive picture. This might include employee engagement surveys, turnover metrics, productivity data, focus groups, and one-on-one conversations. The goal is to identify specific behaviors, processes, or cultural norms that are creating the drag on the Flywheel.

For instance, a manufacturing company might discover that a long-standing practice of publicly comparing individual performance metrics creates anxiety and resentment among workers, slowing the Flywheel's rotation.

3. *Reframe Mindsets and Expectations*

With a clear understanding of the current state, leaders can begin to articulate a compelling vision for a more positive future state. This reframing is crucial for changing the direction of the Flywheel's spin from negative to positive. Reframing involves shifting from a scarcity mindset focused on problems and limitations to an abundance mindset concentrating on possibilities and strengths. Leaders must consciously model this shift in their language and attitude, looking for opportunities to highlight what's working well and approaching challenges with curiosity rather than blame. For example, a healthcare organization might reframe budget constraints from a threat to an opportunity for innovation in care delivery.

This positive orientation can become contagious, gradually changing the tone of workplace interactions, and adding momentum to the Positivity Flywheel.

4. *Cultivate Psychological Capital*

Psychological capital (PsyCap)—comprising hope, efficacy, resilience, and optimism—fuels the Positive Flywheel. Leaders cultivate these qualities in individuals and teams to ensure a steady supply of positive energy to maintain the Flywheel's momentum. Leaders can foster PsyCap through targeted training programs, coaching, and creating an environment that nurtures these qualities. For instance, they build hope by involving employees in goal setting and helping them map out pathways to achieve those goals. They can develop resilience by reframing setbacks such as learning opportunities and celebrating efforts to overcome challenges, adding speed to the Positivity Flywheel.

5. *Address Negativity Constructively*

Even as the Positivity Flywheel gains momentum, pockets of negativity may persist. Addressing these constructively is crucial to prevent them from creating a drag on the system. This step involves creating processes for surfacing and resolving issues productively.

Leaders should foster psychological safety so people can voice concerns openly and provide training in healthy conflict-resolution skills. They must also be willing to engage directly with sources of negativity rather than avoiding them and have difficult conversations when necessary.

For example, a retail organization might implement a structured process for employees to submit improvement suggestions and commit to responding to every submission within a specific timeframe. This demonstrates that leadership takes concerns seriously and is committed to continuous improvement.

6. *Reinforce Positivity and Celebrate Success*

As the Positivity Flywheel picks up speed, it's essential to reinforce positive norms and behaviors to maintain its momentum continually. This involves consistently recognizing and rewarding actions that align with the desired culture. Celebration is a powerful tool for reinforcement. This can take many forms, from public recognition in team meetings to formal award programs to impromptu expressions of gratitude. The key is making the celebration a regular, integral part of organizational life. A financial services firm might implement a digital "kudos" system where employees can give each other points for helpful actions, redeemable for small rewards. This would increase peer-to-peer recognition and provide data on where positive behaviors are taking hold, allowing leaders to amplify, and spread these practices.

The 6-step framework and the Positivity Flywheel metaphor work together synergistically. The framework provides a structured approach for leaders to follow, while the flywheel concept helps visualize the cumulative impact of these efforts over time.

As leaders progress through the framework steps, they add energy to the Positivity Flywheel, increasing its rotational speed. Each step addresses a different aspect of organizational culture, ensuring a comprehensive approach to transformation:

* Authentic leadership and recognizing negativity's impact help overcome initial inertia.
* Reframing mindsets and cultivating psychological capital provide the energy to accelerate the Flywheel's rotation.
* Addressing negativity constructively removes obstacles that could slow the Flywheel down.
* Reinforcing positivity and celebrating success maintains the Flywheel's momentum over time.

It's important to note that this is not a linear process. Leaders must often cycle through these steps multiple times, adjusting their approach based on feedback and results. The Flywheel may sometimes slow down or encounter resistance, requiring renewed focus on earlier steps in the framework.

Challenges and Resistance

Implementing this integrated approach to cultural transformation is challenging. Common obstacles include:

1. Entrenched negative mindsets: People habituated to negativity may initially resist efforts to shift the culture, viewing positivity initiatives as naive or insincere.
2. Lack of trust: Employees may be skeptical of new initiatives if there's a history of failed change efforts or breached promises.
3. Middle management bottleneck: Cultural change often energizes frontline employees and senior leaders, but middle managers may need help translating it 4. into day-to-day practices.
5. External pressures: Market challenges, regulatory constraints, or other external factors can create stress that makes it difficult to maintain positivity.
6. Impatience for results: Cultural change takes time, and some stakeholders may get frustrated if they don't see immediate improvements.
Conflicting subcultures: Different departments or locations may have developed distinct subcultures that are challenging to align.

Navigating these challenges requires persistence, adaptability, and a systems-thinking approach. Leaders need to anticipate and plan for resistance while remaining open to feedback that may highlight legitimate concerns or blind spots in the change approach.

Measuring Progress and Impact

Measuring the impact of cultural transformation efforts is crucial for maintaining accountability and guiding ongoing efforts. A holistic measurement approach should include both quantitative and qualitative indicators.

Quantitative metrics might include:

* Employee engagement scores
* Turnover rates
* Productivity measures

* Customer satisfaction ratings
* Financial performance indicators

Qualitative indicators could involve:

* Sentiment analysis of internal communications
* Observational data on meeting dynamics and decision-making processes
* Employee focus groups and interviews
* Leadership behavior assessments

These metrics help leaders gauge the speed and stability of the Positivity Flywheel, identifying areas where additional energy or intervention may be needed.

Conclusion

The Positivity Flywheel metaphor, combined with the six-step framework for cultural transformation, provides a powerful approach for leaders seeking to shift their organizations from negativity to positivity. By understanding the mechanics of the Flywheel—what starts it, keeps it spinning, and what might slow it down—leaders can more effectively navigate the complex journey of cultural change.

This comprehensive approach recognizes that sustainable transformation requires consistent effort across multiple dimensions of organizational life. It's not about quick fixes or surface-level changes but fundamentally reshaping how people think, feel, and behave at work.

The Positivity Flywheel gains momentum and creates a self-reinforcing cycle of positive change. Employees become more engaged and innovative, attracting like-minded talent, and building a reputation that sets the organization apart in the marketplace. This positive momentum provides resilience in the face of challenges and a solid foundation for long-term success.

Creating a positive organizational culture is not just about improving performance metrics. It's about building workplaces where people can thrive, find meaning in their work, and contribute their best efforts toward a shared purpose. In a world facing unprecedented challenges, such positive, resilient organizations are more important than ever.

Cultural transformation is an ongoing journey that requires continuous attention and refinement. However, by leveraging the power of the Positivity Flywheel and following the holistic 6-step framework, leaders can create lasting positive change that benefits their employees, their organizations, and society.

Recap: The Positivity Flywheel

The Positivity Flywheel depicts how positive organizational changes build upon each other, creating momentum for cultural transformation. It requires initial effort from leaders but becomes self-sustaining over time. The flywheel integrates with the SPIRAL 6-step framework to guide leaders in shifting their organizations towards positivity.

Key Insights:

* Cultural transformation is a cyclical process, not a linear journey.
* The Positivity Flywheel represents the accumulation and momentum of positive cultural elements.
* Trust, psychological safety, engagement, and purpose are crucial components of the Positivity Flywheel.
* Authentic leadership is essential for initiating and maintaining the Flywheel's momentum.
* Addressing negativity constructively is crucial to prevent drag on the system.
* Celebration and reinforcement of positive behaviors are crucial to sustaining momentum.
* An integrated approach, combining the Positivity Flywheel concept with a structured framework, is most effective for cultural transformation.

5 Leadership Reflection Questions:

1. How am I currently contributing to or hindering the momentum of our organization's Positivity Flywheel?

2. How can I more authentically model the positive cultural changes I want to see in my team?

3. What are our organization's primary sources of negativity, and how can I address them constructively?

4. How effectively am I cultivating my team's psychological capital (hope, efficacy, resilience, optimism)?

5. What systems or processes in our organization might unintentionally slow down our Positivity Flywheel?

Leadership Challenge:

Over the next month, implement a daily practice of recognizing and celebrating small wins within your team. Keep a journal of how this impacts team morale, productivity, and your leadership approach. At the end of the month, reflect on how this practice has influenced the momentum of your team's Positivity Flywheel.

Team Discussion Exercise: Flywheel Mapping Activity

<u>Objective</u>: To collaboratively identify the components of your team's Positivity Flywheel and strategies to keep it spinning.

<u>Steps</u>:
1. Draw a large circle on a whiteboard or shared digital space to represent your team's Flywheel.

2. Have team members brainstorm and write down the positive elements that contribute to your team's success and culture on sticky notes.

3. Categorize these elements and place them around the Flywheel.

4. Discuss as a group:

    - Which elements are most vital in your team?

    - Which needs more development?

    - How do these elements reinforce each other?

5. Identify potential "friction points" that might slow down your Flywheel.

6. Brainstorm strategies to address these friction points and further strengthen the positive elements.

7. Create an action plan with specific steps to implement these strategies over the next quarter.

8. Schedule a follow-up meeting to review progress and adjust the plan as needed.

This exercise helps teams visualize their Positivity Flywheel, fostering a shared understanding of what drives positive momentum and how to maintain it.

Appendix I: Definition of Terms

1. **Abundance Mindset** (Ch. 5, 9): A perspective that there are enough resources and opportunities for everyone.

2. **Active Listening** (Ch. 7): Fully concentrating on, understanding, responding to, and remembering what is being said.

3. **Adaptive Leadership**: A leadership approach that emphasizes the ability to adapt to changing environments and challenges. (Not explicitly referenced in specific chapters)

4. **Allostatic Load**: The physiological consequences of chronic exposure to elevated or fluctuating stress hormones. (Related to discussions in Ch. 4)

5. **Amygdala Hijack**: An emotional response that bypasses the rational part of the brain, leading to immediate, often exaggerated reactions. (Related to discussions in Ch. 4)

6. **Appreciative Inquiry** (Ch. 7, 10): A strength-based approach to organizational change that focuses on identifying and amplifying what works well.

7. **Attribution Theory**: Explains *how* individuals interpret events and how this relates to their thinking and behavior. (Related to discussions in Ch. 5)

8. **Authentic Leadership** (Ch. 2, 3, 9): A leadership approach characterized by self-awareness, relational transparency, balanced processing, and internalized moral perspective.

9. **Autonomy Support**: Providing individuals with choice, rationale, and opportunities for self-direction. (Related to discussions in Ch. 6)

10. **Behavioral Contagion** (Ch. 1, 8): The tendency for behaviors and attitudes to spread from person to person within a group.

11. **Broaden-and-Build Theory** (Ch. 1): A theory proposing that positive emotions broaden one's awareness and encourage novel thoughts and actions.

12. **Cognitive Dissonance**: The mental discomfort experienced when holding contradictory beliefs or values. (Related to discussions in Ch. 5)

13. **Cognitive Reframing** (Ch. 5, 6): The process of deliberately shifting one's perspective to view a situation in a different, often more positive light.

14. **Collective Efficacy**: A group's shared belief in its ability to organize and execute actions required to achieve goals. (Related to discussions in Ch. 6)

15. **Confirmation Bias**: The tendency to search for, interpret, favor, and recall information that confirms or supports one's prior beliefs or values. (Related to discussions in Ch. 5)

16. **Continuous Improvement** (Ch. 10): An ongoing effort to improve products, services, or processes over time.

17. **Cortisol** (Ch. 4): A hormone released in response to stress, often referred to as the "stress hormone."

18. **Cultural Intelligence**: The capability to relate and work effectively across cultures. (Related to discussions in Ch. 2)

19. **Cultural Transformation** (Ch. 9, 10): The process of comprehensively changing the values, beliefs, attitudes, and behaviors that characterize an organization.

20. **Default Mode Network**: A network of brain regions active when an individual is not focused on the outside world. (Related to discussions in Ch. 4)

21. **Diffusion of Responsibility**: The tendency for people to take less responsibility for their actions when others are present. (Related to discussions in Ch. 7)

22. **Dunning-Kruger Effect**: A cognitive bias in which people with limited knowledge or competence in a given domain overestimate their own knowledge or competence. (Related to discussions in Ch. 5)

23. **Emotional Contagion** (Ch. 1, 8): The phenomenon where emotions spread from one person to another within a group.

24. **Emotional Intelligence** (Ch. 3, 7): The ability to recognize, understand, and manage one's own emotions and those of others.

25. **Employee Engagement** (Ch. 6, 8, 9): The level of an employee's commitment to and involvement in their organization and its goals.

26. **Eustress**: Beneficial stress that motivates and focuses energy. (Related to discussions in Ch. 4)

27. **Experimental Learning Theory**: A theory that emphasizes the central role of experience in the learning process. (Related to discussions in Ch. 6)

28. **Fixed Mindset** (Ch. 5): The belief that abilities and intelligence are static and unchangeable.

29. **Flow State** (Ch. 8): A mental state of complete absorption in an activity, characterized by energized focus and enjoyment.

30. **Fundamental Attribution Error**: The tendency to attribute others' behaviors to their personality while attributing our own to external circumstances. (Related to discussions in Ch. 5)

31. **Growth Mindset** (Ch. 5, 9): The belief that abilities and intelligence can be developed through effort, learning, and persistence.

32. **Hedonic Adaptation**: The tendency of humans to quickly return to a relatively stable level of happiness despite major positive or negative events. (Related to discussions in Ch. 6)

33. **HERO** (Hope, Efficacy, Resilience, Optimism) (Ch. 6, 9): The four components of psychological capital.

34. **Impostor Syndrome**: A psychological pattern in which an individual doubts their skills and accomplishments and has a persistent fear of being exposed as a "fraud". (Related to discussions in Ch. 5)

35. ***Inside Out* 2** (movie reference) (Ch. 4): An animated film used as a metaphor for understanding emotions and mental processes.

36. **Interpersonal Neurobiology** (Ch. 4): An interdisciplinary field exploring how relationships shape the brain and mind.

37. **Leadership Development** (Ch. 9, 10): The process of improving and expanding the capabilities of leaders within an organization.

38. **Learned Helplessness** (Ch. 7): A condition where a person believes they have no control over their situation and thus gives up trying.

39. **Learned Optimism** (Ch. 5, 6): The idea that an optimistic outlook can be cultivated through specific cognitive techniques.

40. **Life Minded vs. Death Minded** (Ch. 5): Contrasting perspectives focusing on growth and possibilities versus limitations and adverse outcomes.

41. **Limbic Resonance**: The ability of mammals to share deep emotional states. (Related to discussions in Ch. 1)

42. **Maslow's Hierarchy of Needs**: A theory of motivation based on a hierarchy of human needs. (Related to discussions in Ch. 6)

43. **Mindfulness** (Ch. 6, 7): The practice of maintaining awareness of one's thoughts, feelings, and surroundings in the present moment.

44. **Mirror Neurons** (Ch. 1): Brain cells that fire both when an animal acts and when it observes the same action performed by another.

45. **Negativity Bias** (Ch. 1, 2, 4, 9): The psychological tendency to give greater weight to negative experiences than to positive ones.

46. **Negativity Spiral** (Ch. 4, 9): A self-reinforcing cycle where negative thoughts and behaviors lead to more negativity.

47. **Neurodiversity**: The concept that neurological differences are to be recognized and respected as any other human variation. (Related to discussions in Ch. 2)

48. **Neuroplasticity** (Ch. 4): The brain's ability to form and reorganize synaptic connections, especially in response to learning or experience.

49. **No Asshole Rule** (Ch. 1, 3): A concept emphasizing the importance of not tolerating toxic behavior in the workplace.

50. **Organizational Culture** (Ch. 2, 9, 10): The shared values, beliefs, and practices that characterize an organization.

51. **Peer Advisory Groups** (Ch. 9): Groups of professionals who meet regularly to share advice and support each other's development.

52. **PERMA Model** (Ch. 10): A model of well-being that includes Positive emotions, Engagement, Relationships, Meaning, and Accomplishment.

53. **Positive Deviance** (Ch. 7, 9): An approach to behavioral and social change based on the observation that in any community, there are people whose uncommon practices enable them to find better solutions to problems than their peers.

54. **Positive Organizational Scholarship** (Ch. 9, 10): The study of positive outcomes, processes, and attributes of organizations and their members.

55. **Positivity Flywheel** (Bonus Chapter, Ch. 10): A metaphor representing the accumulation and momentum of positive cultural elements in an organization.

56. **Psychological Capital** (PsyCap) (Ch. 2, 6, 9): An individual's positive psychological state characterized by hope, efficacy, resilience, and optimism.

57. **Psychological Safety** (Ch. 3, 7, 9): An environment where people feel safe to take interpersonal risks, such as speaking up or offering ideas.

58. **Response Styles Theory** (Ch. 1): A theory proposing that the way people respond to negative moods influences the duration of those moods.

59. **Scarcity Mindset** (Ch. 5, 9): The belief that there are never enough resources, leading to negative emotions and unproductive behavior.

60. **Self-Efficacy** (Ch. 6, 9): An individual's belief in their capacity to execute behaviors necessary to produce specific performance attainments.

61. **Sentiment Analysis** (Ch. 10): The use of natural language processing to systematically identify and extract subjective information from text.

62. **Social Modeling** (Ch. 6): Learning that occurs through observing the behavior of others.

63. **Spiral Up Framework** (Ch. 9, 10): A six-step approach to transforming organizational culture from negativity to positivity.

64. **Strengths-Based Approach** (Ch. 6, 10): A perspective focusing on identifying and developing individuals' inherent talents and capabilities.

65. **Stress Inoculation** (Ch. 6): A form of cognitive behavioral therapy aimed at helping people prepare themselves in advance to handle stressful events successfully.

66. **Surviving vs. Thriving** (Ch. 5, 9): Contrasting states of merely coping with challenges versus flourishing and growing.

67. **Systems Thinking** (Ch. 9, 10): An approach to analysis that focuses on how parts of a system interrelate and how systems work over time and within larger systems.

68. **Toxic Culture** (Ch. 1, 2, 4): An organizational environment characterized by negativity, dysfunction, and harmful behaviors.

69. **Transparency in Leadership** (Ch. 3, 7): The practice of being open and honest in communication and decision-making processes.

70. **VUCA** (Volatile, Uncertain, Complex, Ambiguous) (Ch. 5): An acronym describing the challenging nature of the modern business environment.

Appendix II: Executive Interview Profile Chart

Demographic Characteristics of Participants

Table 1 - Demographic Characteristics of Participants

Alias	Gender	Roles	Years in Role	Industry
EX01	F	CPO*	5	Financial
EX02	F	Executive Director	3	Education
EX03	F	Project Executive	5	Construction
EX04	M	CEO	5	Agriculture
EX05	M	CEO	4	Non-Profit
EX06	M	CEO	10+	Non-Profit
EX07	F	CPO	5	Senior Living
EX08	M	CEO	10+	Education
EX09	M	CEO	7	Healthcare
EX10	F	CPO	1	Construction
EX11	M	CEO	10+	Construction

* Chief People Officer

Note:
CEO-Chief Executive Officer
COO-Chief Operations Officer
CPO-Chief People Officer

Appendix III: Pre-work Questions for Consulting Engagement

1. **Cultural Assessment**
   - How would you describe your current organizational culture?
   - What are the primary sources of negativity or challenges in your workplace?
   - How have past culture change efforts succeeded or fallen short?
2. **Leadership Readiness**
   - How committed is your executive team to cultural transformation?
   - What personal development work have leaders undertaken to prepare for this journey?
   - How open is leadership to feedback and new approaches?
3. **Organizational Context**
   - What significant business challenges or changes is your organization facing?
   - How might industry trends or market forces impact cultural transformation efforts?
   - What unique strengths or assets can you leverage in this process?
4. **Employee Engagement**
   - How would you characterize current levels of employee engagement and morale?
   - What mechanisms exist for gathering employee feedback and ideas?
   - How ready is your workforce for a cultural shift towards greater positivity?
5. **Systems and Processes**
   - Which organizational systems might be inadvertently reinforcing negativity?
   - What current initiatives or programs align to foster positivity?

- How integrated are your various people processes (hiring, onboarding, performance management, etc.)?

6. Measurement and Accountability

- What metrics do you currently use to assess cultural health and employee wellbeing?

- How are leaders held accountable for their impact on organizational culture?

- What would success look like for this cultural transformation effort?

7. Resources and Constraints

- What resources (time, budget, personnel) are available for this transformation effort?

- What potential obstacles or resistance do you anticipate?

- How will this work be prioritized alongside other organizational initiatives?

8. Vision and Values

- What is your aspiration for your organization's culture?

- How well-defined and lived are your current organizational values?

- How might a shift towards greater positivity support your broader business strategy?

References

Chapter 1

1. Avey, James B., Fred Luthans, and Susan M. Jensen. "Psychological Capital: A Positive Resource for Combating Employee Stress and Turnover." Human Resource Management 48, no. 5 (2009): 677-693.

2. Avolio, Bruce J., and William L. Gardner. "Authentic Leadership Development: Getting to the Root of Positive Forms of Leadership." The Leadership Quarterly 16, no. 3 (2005): 315-338.

3. Barsade, Sigal G. "The Ripple Effect: Emotional Contagion and Its Influence on Group Behavior." Administrative Science Quarterly 47, no. 4 (2002): 644-675.

4. Baumeister, Roy F., Ellen Bratslavsky, Catrin Finkenauer, and Kathleen D. Vohs. "Bad Is Stronger Than Good." Review of General Psychology 5, no. 4 (2001): 323-370.

5. Corns, Jennifer. "Rethinking the Negativity Bias." Review of Philosophy and Psychology 9, no. 3 (2018): 607-625.

6. Felps, Will, Terence R. Mitchell, and Eliza Byington. "How, When, and Why Bad Apples Spoil the Barrel: Negative Group Members and Dysfunctional Groups." Research in Organizational Behavior 27 (2006): 175-222.

7. Fredrickson, Barbara L. "The Role of Positive Emotions in Positive Psychology: The Broaden-and-Build Theory of Positive Emotions." American Psychologist 56, no. 3 (2001): 218-226.

8. Fredrickson, Barbara L., and Thomas Joiner. "Positive Emotions Trigger Upward Spirals Toward Emotional Well-Being." Psychological Science 13, no. 2 (2002): 172-175.

9. Gottman, John M. What Predicts Divorce?: The Relationship Between Marital Processes and Marital Outcomes. Hillsdale, NJ: Lawrence Erlbaum Associates, 1994.

10. Kaplan, Seth A., Jose Cortina, Gregory A. Ruark, Kate E. LaPort, and Vias Nicolaides. "The Role of Organizational Leaders in Employee Emotion Management: A Theoretical Model." The Leadership Quarterly 25, no. 3 (2014): 563-580.

11. Nolen-Hoeksema, Susan. "Responses to Depression and Their Effects on the Duration of Depressive Episodes." Journal of Abnormal Psychology 100, no. 4 (1991): 569-582.

12. Rozin, Paul, and Edward B. Royzman. "Negativity Bias, Negativity Dominance, and Contagion." Personality and Social Psychology Review 5, no. 4 (2001): 296-320.

13. Sutton, Robert I. The No Asshole Rule: Building a Civilized Workplace and Surviving One That Isn't. New York: Warner Business Books, 2007.

14. Vaish, Amrisha, Tobias Grossmann, and Amanda Woodward. "Not All Emotions Are Created Equal: The Negativity Bias in Social-Emotional Development." Psychological Bulletin 134, no. 3 (2008): 383-403.

Chapter 2

1. Alvesson, Mats, and Katja Einola. "Warning for Excessive Positivity:

Authentic Leadership and Other Traps in Leadership Studies." The Leadership Quarterly 30, no. 4 (2019): 383-395.

2. Avolio, Bruce J., and William L. Gardner. "Authentic Leadership Development: Getting to the Root of Positive Forms of Leadership." The Leadership Quarterly 16, no. 3 (2005): 315-338.

3. Charmaz, Kathy. Constructing Grounded Theory. 2nd ed. London: SAGE Publications, 2014.

4. George, Bill, Peter Sims, Andrew N. McLean, and Diana Mayer. "Discovering Your Authentic Leadership." Harvard Business Review 85, no. 2 (2007): 129-138.

5. Gesser-Edelsburg, Anat, Nour Abed Elhadi Shahbari, Ricky Cohen, Adva Mir Halavi, Rana Hijazi, Galit Paz-Yaakobovitch, Yehudith Birman-Shemesh, and Huda Daoud Hajoj. "Differences in Perceptions of Health Information Between the Public and Health Care Professionals: Nonprobability Sampling Questionnaire Survey." Journal of Medical Internet Research 21, no. 7 (2019): e14105.

6. Ibarra, Herminia. "The Authenticity Paradox." Harvard Business Review 93, no. 1/2 (2015): 52-59.

7. Ladkin, Donna, and Steven S. Taylor. "Enacting the 'True Self': Towards a Theory of Embodied Authentic Leadership." The Leadership Quarterly 21, no. 1 (2010): 64-74.

8. Leroy, Hannes, Ans De Vos, and Yves Segers. "Authentic Leadership, Authentic Followership, Basic Need Satisfaction, and Work Role Performance: A Cross-Level Study." Journal of Management 41, no. 6 (2015): 1677-1697.

9. Nyberg, Daniel, and Stefan Sveningsson. "Paradoxes of Authentic Leadership: Leader Identity Struggles." Leadership 10, no. 4 (2014): 437-455.

10. Tourish, Dennis. "Is Complexity Leadership Theory Complex Enough? A Critical Appraisal, Some Modifications and Suggestions for Further Research." Organization Studies 40, no. 2 (2019): 219-238.

11. Walumbwa, Fred O., Bruce J. Avolio, William L. Gardner, Tara S. Wernsing, and Suzanne J. Peterson. "Authentic Leadership: Development and Validation of a Theory-Based Measure." Journal of Management 34, no. 1 (2008): 89-126.

Chapter 3

1. Avolio, Bruce J., William L. Gardner, Fred O. Walumbwa, Fred Luthans, and Douglas R. May. "Unlocking the Mask: A Look at the Process by Which Authentic Leaders Impact Follower Attitudes and Behaviors." The Leadership Quarterly 15, no. 6 (2004): 801-823.

2. Boyd, Brady. Life Minded: Living with Purpose and Perspective. Nashville: W Publishing Group, 2022.

3. Dweck, Carol S. "Mindset: The New Psychology of Success." New York: Random House, 2006.

4. Gardner, William L., Claudia C. Cogliser, Kelley M. Davis, and Matthew P. Dickens. "Authentic Leadership: A Review of the Literature and Research Agenda." The Leadership Quarterly 22, no. 6 (2011): 1120-1145.

5. Sutton, Robert I. Good Boss, Bad Boss: How to Be the Best... and Learn from the Worst. New York: Business Plus, 2010.

6. Sutton, Robert I. The No Asshole Rule: Building a Civilized Workplace and Surviving One That Isn't. New York: Warner Business Books, 2007.

Chapter 4

1. Kaplan, Seth A., Jose Cortina, Gregory A. Ruark, Kate E. LaPort, and Vias Nicolaides. "The Role of Organizational Leaders in Employee Emotion Management: A Theoretical Model." The Leadership Quarterly 25, no. 3 (2014): 563-580.

2. Kuzior, Aleksandra, Bartosz Sobotka, and Dagmara Zwierzchowska. "The Role of Social Capital and Organizational Trust in Corporate Governance." Sustainability 14, no. 17 (2022): 10448.

3. Landolfi, Attila, Agota G. Szabo, and Zoltan Adrovicz. "Interpersonal Conflicts During the COVID-19 Pandemic: The Role of Personality Traits." Personality and Individual Differences 179 (2021): 110913.

4. Wax, Rotem Shneor, Inbal Nahum-Shani, and Anat Rafaeli. "Workplace Negativity: Causes, Consequences, and Solutions." Annual Review of Organizational Psychology and Organizational Behavior 9 (2022): 379-406.

Chapter 5

1. Lyubomirsky, Sonja, Laura King, and Ed Diener. "The Benefits of Frequent Positive Affect: Does Happiness Lead to Success?" Psychological Bulletin 131, no. 6 (2005): 803-855.

2. Mullainathan, Sendhil, and Eldar Shafir. Scarcity: Why Having Too Little Means So Much. New York: Times Books, 2013.

3. Robertson, Kelley. "Active Listening: More Than Just Paying Attention." Australian Family Physician 34, no. 12 (2005): 1053-1055.

4. Seligman, Martin E. P. Learned Optimism: How to Change Your Mind and Your Life. New York: Knopf, 1991.

5. Spreitzer, Gretchen, and Christine Porath. "Creating Sustainable Performance." Harvard Business Review 90, no. 1-2 (2012): 92-99.

Chapter 6

1. Avey, James B., Rebecca J. Reichard, Fred Luthans, and Ketan H. Mhatre. "Meta-Analysis of the Impact of Positive Psychological Capital on Employee Attitudes, Behaviors, and Performance." Human Resource Development Quarterly 22, no. 2 (2011): 127-152.

2. Ciftci, Dilek Ozer, and Huseyin Erkanli. "Mediating Role of Positive Psychological Capital in Relationship Between Authentic Leadership and Psychological Contract Breach." Journal of Positive Psychology and Wellbeing 4, no. 1 (2020): 86-101.

3. Luthans, Fred, Carolyn M. Youssef, and Bruce J. Avolio. Psychological Capital: Developing the Human Competitive Edge. Oxford: Oxford University Press, 2007.

4. Niswaty, Risma, Rudi Salam, and Muhammad Darwis. "The Effect of Authentic Leadership on Work Engagement: The Mediating Role of Psychological Capital." International Journal of Instruction 14, no. 3 (2021): 969-986.

5. Saeed, Munaza, Sharjeel Saleem, and Shazia Nauman. "Psychological Capital, Work Engagement and Burnout: A Systematic Review and Meta-Analysis." International Journal of Environmental Research and Public Health 20, no. 4 (2023): 3360.

6. Shahid, Shadab, and Michael K. Muchiri. "Positivity at the Workplace: Conceptualizing the Relationships Between Authentic Leadership, Psychological Capital, Organizational Virtuousness, Thriving and Job Performance." International Journal of Organizational Analysis 27, no. 3 (2019): 494-523.

Chapter 7

1. Allio, Robert J. "The Practical Strategist: Business and Corporate Strategy for the 1990s." New York: Praeger, 1988.

2. Block, Peter. Flawless Consulting: A Guide to Getting Your Expertise Used. 3rd ed. San Francisco: Pfeiffer, 2011.

3. Cooperrider, David L., and Michelle McQuaid. "The Positive Arc of Systemic Strengths: How Appreciative Inquiry and Sustainable Designing Can Bring Out the Best in Human Systems." The Journal of Corporate Citizenship, no. 46 (2012): 71-102.

4. Gesser-Edelsburg, Anat, Nour Abed Elhadi Shahbari, Ricky Cohen, Adva Mir Halavi, Rana Hijazi, Galit Paz-Yaakobovitch, Yehudith Birman-Shemesh, and Huda Daoud Hajoj. "Differences in Perceptions of Health Information Between the Public and Health Care Professionals: Nonprobability Sampling Questionnaire Survey." Journal of Medical Internet Research 21, no. 7 (2019): e14105.

Chapter 8

1. Brown, Stuart. Play: How it Shapes the Brain, Opens the Imagination, and Invigorates the Soul. New York: Avery, 2009.

2. Cameron, Kim S., Jane E. Dutton, and Robert E. Quinn, eds. Positive Organizational Scholarship: Foundations of a New Discipline. San Francisco: Berrett-Koehler, 2003.

3. Center for Creative Leadership. "The 3 Types of Developmental Assignments." Accessed August 22, 2024. https://www.ccl.org/articles/leading-effectively-articles/the-3-types-of-developmental-assignments/.

4. Cooperrider, David L., and Michelle McQuaid. "The Positive Arc of

Systemic Strengths: How Appreciative Inquiry and Sustainable Designing Can Bring Out the Best in Human Systems." The Journal of Corporate Citizenship, no. 46 (2012): 71-102.

5. Csikszentmihalyi, Mihaly. Flow: The Psychology of Optimal Experience. New York: Harper & Row, 1990.

6. Gallup. "Employee Recognition: Low Cost, High Impact." Accessed August 22, 2024. https://www.gallup.com/workplace/236441/employee-recognition-low-cost-high-impact.aspx.

7. Price, Catherine. The Power of Fun: How to Feel Alive Again. New York: Dial Press, 2021.

8. Sinek, Simon. Leaders Eat Last: Why Some Teams Pull Together and Others Don't. New York: Portfolio/Penguin, 2014.

Chapter 9

1. Avey, James B., Rebecca J. Reichard, Fred Luthans, and Ketan H. Mhatre. "Meta-Analysis of the Impact of Positive Psychological Capital on Employee Attitudes, Behaviors, and Performance." Human Resource Development Quarterly 22, no. 2 (2011): 127-152.

2. Cameron, Kim S., and Gretchen M. Spreitzer, eds. The Oxford Handbook of Positive Organizational Scholarship. New York: Oxford University Press, 2012.

3. Dweck, Carol S. "Mindset: The New Psychology of Success." Random House Digital, Inc., 2008.

4. Gallo, Amy. "How to Manage a Toxic Employee." Harvard Business Review, October 3, 2016. https://hbr.org/2016/10/how-to-manage-a-toxic-employee.

5. International Coach Federation. "2009 ICF Global Coaching Client Study." Lexington, KY: International Coach Federation, 2009.

6. Luthans, Fred, Carolyn M. Youssef, and Bruce J. Avolio. Psychological Capital: Developing the Human Competitive Edge. Oxford: Oxford University Press, 2007.

7. McDonald, Michael L., and James D. Westphal. "Getting by with the Advice of Their Friends: CEOs' Advice Networks and Firms' Strategic Responses to Poor Performance." Administrative Science Quarterly 48, no. 1 (2003): 1-32.

8. Petrie, Nick. "Future Trends in Leadership Development." Center for Creative Leadership, 2014.

9. Yip, Jeffrey, and Meena S. Wilson. "Learning from Experience." In The Center for Creative Leadership Handbook of Leadership Development, edited by Ellen Van Velsor, Cynthia D. McCauley, and Marian N. Ruderman, 63-95. San Francisco: Jossey-Bass, 2010.

Chapter 10

1. Avey, James B., Rebecca J. Reichard, Fred Luthans, and Ketan H. Mhatre. "Meta-Analysis of the Impact of Positive Psychological Capital on Employee Attitudes, Behaviors, and Performance." Human Resource Development Quarterly 22, no. 2 (2011): 127-152.

2. Cameron, Kim S., Jane E. Dutton, and Robert E. Quinn, eds. Positive Organizational Scholarship: Foundations of a New Discipline. San Francisco: Berrett-Koehler, 2003.

3. Fredrickson, Barbara L. "The Value of Positive Emotions: The Emerging Science of Positive Psychology is Coming to Understand Why It's Good to Feel Good." American Scientist 91, no. 4 (2003): 330-335.

4. Luthans, Fred, Carolyn M. Youssef, and Bruce J. Avolio. Psychological Capital: Developing the Human Competitive Edge. Oxford: Oxford University Press, 2007.

Bonus Chapter: The Positivity Flywheel

1. Avolio, Bruce J., William L. Gardner, Fred O. Walumbwa, Fred Luthans, and Douglas R. May. "Unlocking the Mask: A Look at the Process by Which Authentic Leaders Impact Follower Attitudes and Behaviors." The Leadership Quarterly 15, no. 6 (2004): 801-823.

2. Cameron, Kim S., and Gretchen M. Spreitzer, eds. The Oxford Handbook of Positive Organizational Scholarship. New York: Oxford University Press, 2012.

3. Dweck, Carol S. "Mindset: The New Psychology of Success." New York: Random House, 2006.

4. Fredrickson, Barbara L. "The Role of Positive Emotions in Positive Psychology: The Broaden-and-Build Theory of Positive Emotions." American Psychologist 56, no. 3 (2001): 218-226.

5. Luthans, Fred, Carolyn M. Youssef, and Bruce J. Avolio. Psychological Capital: Developing the Human Competitive Edge. Oxford: Oxford University Press, 2007.

6. Seligman, Martin E. P. Learned Optimism: How to Change Your Mind and Your Life. New York: Knopf, 1991.

Acknowledgements

I AM DEEPLY GRATEFUL to the many individuals who have contributed to the creation of this work and supported me throughout this journey.

To the executives who participated in my research process, your insights and experiences have been invaluable. Your willingness to share openly has enriched this work immeasurably.

A special thanks to Marcus Costantino for helping shape the book, providing crucial feedback on the Spiraling Up flow, layout, and practicality for leaders. Your input has been instrumental in making this work accessible and impactful.

To Ed, Mike, Christina, Michael, Toti, Jimmy, and Sandy - your support and contributions have been vital to this project. Thank you for your time, expertise, and encouragement.

I am profoundly grateful to all my coaching clients. Our conversations have helped shape Spiraling Up to serve the next generation of leaders. Your trust in me and your own growth journeys have been a constant source of inspiration.

To my beloved wife, Cari - after 30 years of marriage, you have been my partner in every arena of life. Your unwavering encouragement, support, and love have made it possible to reach this summit. Sharing life with you, through a thousand coffee conversations, has been the schoolroom where I've learned about faith, family, and working with people.

To my children - each of you inspires me! You help me become a better learner. The love and service you show to so many in your friendships, classrooms, productions, and church communities spur me on. You've been my constant cheerleaders. I love being your Dad!

Finally, thank you to my entire family for providing the grace and space for the countless hours in writing Spiraling Up and my doctoral journey. Your patience and understanding have been the foundation upon which this work was built.

This accomplishment is as much yours as it is mine. Thank you all.

About the Author

Dr. Russell Verhey is a leadership mentor, coach, and workplace psychologist with deep roots in entrepreneurship and a passion for developing leaders. Raised in Atlanta in a family construction business, Russell became the first in his family to graduate college. His entrepreneurial spirit led him to found Workspace Solutions in 1996, which he ran until 2011.

Since 2002, Russell has been based in Colorado Springs. He has built a multifaceted career focused on leadership development. He facilitates CEO peer groups, provides executive coaching, and has taught as an adjunct professor at UCCS for several years. As a consultant, Russell has worked with Fortune-level companies to design leadership programs, mentor executives, and reshape organizational cultures. His approach emphasizes positivity and measurable outcomes in employee well-being, productivity, and retention.

Russell earned a master's in leadership from Denver Seminary and a Ph.D. in Industrial-Organizational Psychology from Capella University. He holds multiple coaching certifications and is a member of several professional organizations. In 2016, Russell authored *The Conversationalist*, exploring relationship-building through meaningful dialogue.

Family and faith are central to Russell's life and work. For 15 years, he and his family organized father-child retreats to foster deeper connections. He takes pride in his 30+ year marriage to Cari and their children. An avid outdoors person, Russell enjoys exploring new places, fresh powder skiing, endurance races, and summiting the 58 Colorado fourteeners. He's a decade-long veteran of the 15-minute power nap during the workday and enjoys taking long walks to unwind with his Golden Retriever "grand-puppy" Winston.

Russell on Maroon Peak, 14,163 feet

Dr. Russell Verhey's diverse background, spanning construction, entrepreneurship, organization, and leadership development, uniquely informs his work. His goal is to inspire positive change in leaders and organizations through thoughtful coaching, mentoring, and facilitation. Dr. Verhey's warm personality and 'contagious optimism' have made him a sought-after guide for leaders navigating complex challenges.

THE ADVANCE

Your Partners for Leadership Growth

SINCE 2012, 100S OF ENTREPRENEURS, MANAGERS, AND FORTUNE LEVEL EXECUTIVES HAVE TRUSTED THE ADVANCE TEAM!

COACHING LEADERS | BUILDING TEAMS | CHANGING CULTURE

Advance Executive Coaching

WHO WE'VE SERVED SINCE 2012

ADVANCE YOUR LEADERSHIP!

www.spiralingupleader.com
www.theadvance.net
connect@leadersadvance.net

www.ingramcontent.com/pod-product-compliance
Lightning Source LLC
Chambersburg PA
CBHW070619030426
42337CB00020B/3855